SUN DOWNERS

VF-11 IN WORLD WAR II

By

Barrett Tillman

Aircraft Illustrations
By
John C. Valo

PHALANX
Publishing Co., Ltd.
1051 Marie Avenue
St. Paul, MN 55118 U.S.A.
612/454-0607

Copyright © 1993 by Phalanx Publishing Co., Ltd.

All rights reserved. No part of this work covered by copyright hereon may be reproduced or used in any form or by any means - graphic, electronic, or mechanical, including photocopying, recording, taping or information storage and retrieval systems - without the written permission of the publisher.

ISBN: 0-9625850-8-0

Written by Barrett Tillman

Aircraft profiles by John C. Valo

Maps by Steven Carley

Published by:

Phalanx Publishing Co., Ltd.
1051 Marie Avenue W.
St. Paul, MN 55118-4131 USA

Printed in the United States of America

This Grumman F4F-4 Wildcat, Bureau No. 11985, was the aircraft of Lieutenant William N. Leonard. It carried VF-11 No. F-21. In previous combat with VF-42 and VF-3 operating from carriers Leonard had scored four confirmed kills and one probable. During his Guadalcanal tour with VF-11 he claimed two Zekes, thus recording six meat ball flags on his Wildcat.

A Grumman F6F-5 Hellcat, Bureau No. 94473, of VF-11 operated in the Western Pacific from aircraft carrier, Hornet, CV-12, in late 1944 and 1945. This particular aircraft was inherited from VF-2 where it served a previous combat tour.

ACKNOWLEDGMENTS

The author and the publisher are indebted to many for their assistance in the assembly of this history.

The late Richard M. Hill, himself a former Navy fighter pilot, began gathering work for this history and unselfishly supplied his material. Bill Hess, historian for the American Fighter Aces Association, was helpful as he always is, Charlie Graham supplied photos from his vast collection, and Ben Forrest, one-time Public Affairs Officer for VF-111, provided much post-WW II data.

Mostly we need to acknowledge the assistance of several veteran Sun Downers and their families for their enthusiastic support. They are: C. Barber, VT-11, the late Capt. R.E. Clements, J.J. Crowley, L.J. Ernst, Jr., Rear Adm. E.G. Fairfax, R.N. Flath, Cdr. V.E. Graham, T.H. Holberton, B. Honaker, Rear Adm. W.N. Leonard, Cdr. W.R. Maxwell, Lt. Cdr. H.B. Moranville, Rear Adm. R.E. Riera, R.J. Saggau, the late Capt. J.E. Savage, Mrs. M.B. Stimpson, Capt. J.S. Swope, C.V. Wesley, and the late Cdr. C.M. White.

Despite this throng of contributors, the effort would not have succeeded without the devoted cooperation of Tim Enander, the man who keeps the Sun Downer legend alive.

TABLE OF CONTENTS

Chapter 1	First Tour of Combat	7
Chapter 2	Second Tour of Combat	19

Maps:

Southern Solomon Islands	4
Western Pacific	18
Appendices	42

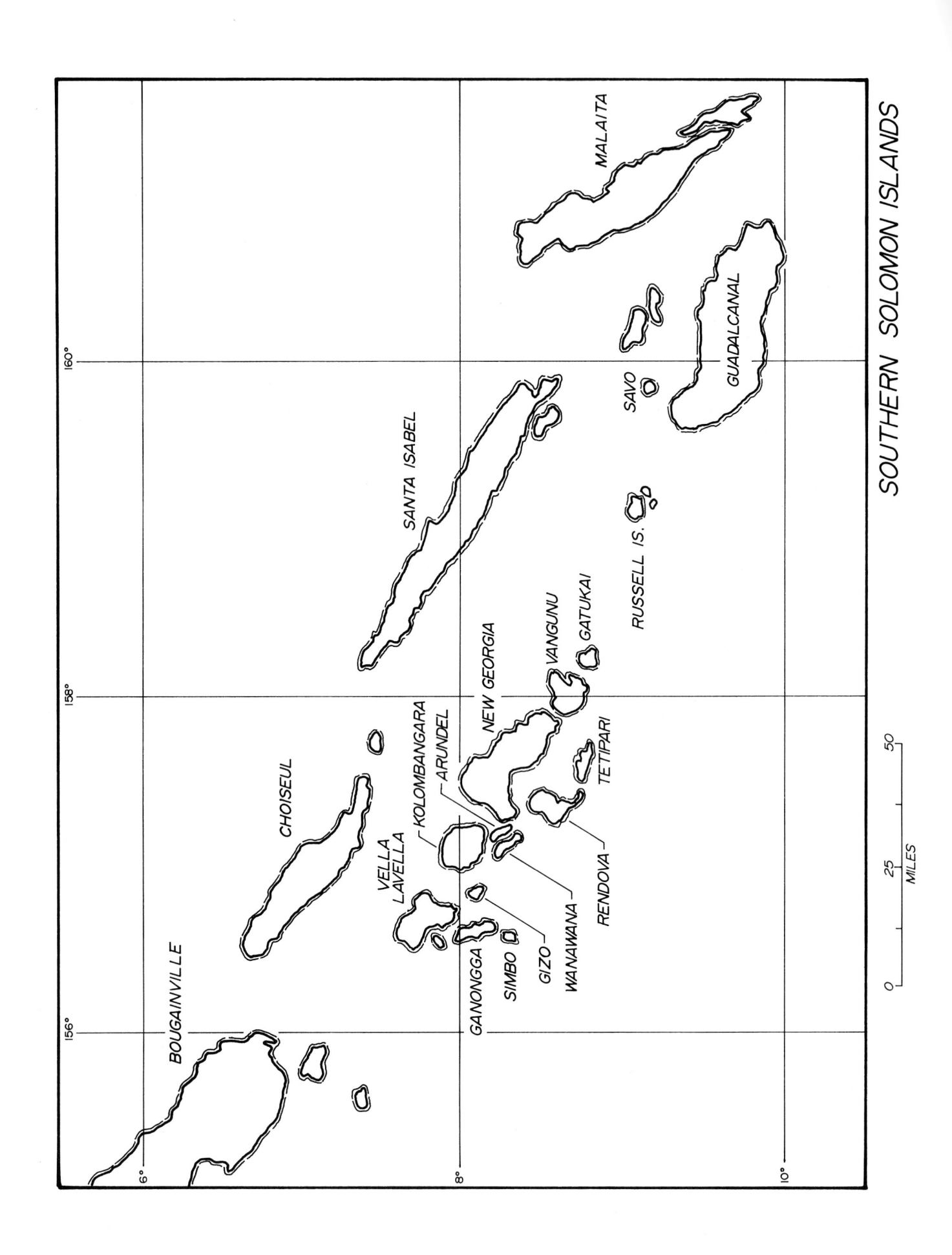

SOUTHERN SOLOMON ISLANDS

FIRST TOUR OF DUTY

A new fighter squadron was being formed at San Diego's North Island Naval Air Station in the first week of August 1942. Commissioning a new unit was nothing unusual at the time, as it was a hectic expansion period for the U.S. Navy. The first American offensive of WW II was barely underway in the Solomon Islands, at a ninety mile long island called Guadalcanal. Since the Battle of the Coral Sea in May the Navy had lost the aircraft carriers **Lexington** and **Yorktown**, putting most of their aviators ashore for reassignment.

North Island's new fighter squadron was designated VF-11. It was the recipient of several displaced pilots, including the commanding officer, Lieutenant Commander Charles R. Fenton. A thirty-five-year-old native of Annapolis, Maryland, Fenton had previously been CO of VF-42 aboard **Yorktown**, sunk at Midway in June. His flight officer, Lieutenant William N. Leonard, was one of the top-scoring carrier pilots from the first phase of the Pacific War. Leonard had four confirmed victories and two probables to his credit while flying with VF-42 and VF-3 at Coral Sea and Midway.

Two other combat-experienced pilots were Lieutenant Frank B. Quady and Lieutenant (jg) Walter J. Hiebert, both formerly of VF-6 aboard **Enterprise**. Quady became the squadron engineering officer while Hiebert took charge of communications. The remaining three senior pilots had seen no combat but were experienced fliers. Lieutenant Clarence M. White, Jr. was designated executive officer and Lieutenant Raymond W. Vogel became operations officer. Lieutenant Gordon D. Cady ran the gunnery department, and VF-11 was fortunate to have him. Cady was developing the boresight gun pattern for the Grumman F4F Wildcat which the squadron flew. But in addition to being experienced aviators, four of VF-11's six senior pilots were graduates of the U.S. Naval Academy. This depth of leadership was unusual.

Fighting Eleven was operating F4F-4s by August 11 and slowly began adding new, younger pilots. When Air Group 11 was commissioned on October 10 under Commander Paul H. Ramsey, Fenton's squadron had about twenty-seven pilots. This included one "white hat," Chief Aviation Pilot Chester A. Parker, who was later commissioned. Future standouts in the squadron were Ensign Jams S. Swope, a tall blond Texan; and Ensign Vernon E. Graham, a rugged good looking Colorado pilot. Ensign Charles R. Stimpson's nickname was "Skull" after his thin appearance, but it would prove appropriate for another reason. Lanky, tough and personable, the twenty-three year old Utah native would become the deadliest of all VF-11 aviators.

After barely two months at North Island, the air group deployed to Hawaii, departing the West Coast on October 23. Most personnel went by transport ship but the more experienced fighter pilots and thirteen Wildcats (half the authorized strength) embarked in the escort carrier **Chenango**. Upon arrival in Hawaii the bomber, scout and torpedo squadrons were based at Barbers Point on Oahu but VF-11 went to NAS Maui, decidedly less crowded.

Fenton began accumulating more aircraft and VF-11 embarked upon a comprehensive training program emphasizing aerial gunnery, strafing, and later "group gropes" with the other squadrons. But it wasn't all work. Fighting Eleven was adopted by a prosperous Maui couple, Boyd and Maria von Tempsky, who operated a large cattle ranch. The von Tempskys had two sons in Europe with the USAAF, and with Boyd's sister Alexa, had become fond of Navy fighter squadrons. Fenton's pilots quickly came to appreciate "the civilized chow, sports, music and other reminders of home," which the estate on the upper slopes of Haleakala Mountain afforded.

While on Maui some of the pilots took steps which are felt today in the squadron's heraldry and terminology. Bill Leonard, Charlie Stimpson and one or two others decided VF-11 should have a squadron insignia, and devised the concept of two stubby Grummans shooting a "rising sun" into the ocean as representative of their mission. With the help of Alexa and Maria the insignia was rendered in color and squadron mechanics devised a multiple stencil system so each Wildcat could have identical emblems. Lieutenant Commander Fenton approved the idea, and thus was born one of the most enduring insignia in U.S. Navy Aviation.

Numerals were not allowed on unit insignia, but along the bottom was printed the legend "Sun Downers," the name by which VF-11 would become popularly known. It referred mainly to the squadron's job of shooting down Japanese "suns," but actually that was only part of the story. "Sundowner" was an old nautical appellation which referred to a diligent worker: a sailor who toiled till day was done. It originated in the days of sail when grog was customarily served on ships, but a strict captain might withhold the ration until dark while others relented when the sun sank below the main yardarm.

Training ended in February, 1943 when the squadron, now filled out with about thirty-five aircraft and forty pilots, boarded **Long Island** and **Altamaha** and

First Row (l to r): Raymond Vogel, Jr., Robert Flath, Robert Maxwell, George Cary (KIA), John Cooke, Charles Fenton, Lowell Slagel, Frederick Graber, Henry White, Frank Quady (KIA), Charles Wesley, Chester Parker. 2nd row: Robert Gilbert, Vernon Graham, William Leonard, George Ricker,(KIA) Clarence White, Jr., James Swope, Charles Stimpson, Nelson Dayhoff (KIA), Edward Johnson, Gordon Cady, Terry Holberton. 3rd Row: Lee Rickabaugh, Bernard Ward, Fordyce Stone, Robert Ogilvie, Walter Hiebert, John Ramsey, Creighton Flynn. 4th Row: Nevance Donaldson, Leslie Ernst, Frank Hynes, Robert Eaton, James Hampton, Lawrence Gersdorf, Walter Duncan, George Dini, Robert McDuffee, John Dugan, Wain Edward Bell. 5th Row: William Herndon, George Archer, Linscott, William Ashton, David Jacobs, Chief Wilson, Orrie Jones, Brown, William Schorre, Lyman Starkey, Edward Uhland. 6th Row: Harold Dailey, Kenneth Boley, Gardner, Lloyd Brouillard, Ernest Hudson, Victory Lentz, John Weimer, Dorrence Haikura. Not shown: Huckabay, Lyons, Rouse, Gaston, Fitzpatrick, Reeves, Enander, Gelmstedt, Hopp, Simmons, Putnam, Perito, Cone, Honaker. Photo was taken at Maui, 1942. (B. Honaker, ID by Haines and Enander)

headed southwest. On March 6 the F4Fs were catapulted off the CVE's short deck for Nandi in the Fiji Islands. The Sun Downers were put on short notice for deployment to Guadalcanal but at almost the same time time lost their skipper, Charlie Fenton. Recalled for duty in Washington, D.C. after six months as C.O., Fenton turned over command to his exec, Clarence White, while Raymond "Sully" Vogel took White's previous job. Bill Leonard assumed the combined duties of flight and operations officer.

The "Tower" and Nandi, Fiji Islands. Personnel Officer, Lt. C.C. Flynn, mans the "biscuit gun" as pilots Frank Quady (center) and Jim Swope kibitz. (Tim Enander)

Air Group 11 was now combat-ready under Commander Weldon L. Hamilton. The pilots were all qualified for carrier operations, but during the period VF-11 spent at North Island the U.S. Navy had lost the services of three more carriers. When the Sun Downers had organized in August and September the early battles around Guadalcanal had sent **Saratoga** to dockyard with torpedo damage and **Wasp** fell prey to a submarine. Then, just days after the air group left San Diego, **Hornet** was lost in the battle of Santa Cruz. By the time Air Group 11 arrived in the combat zone only **Enterprise** remained in combat of the surviving American carriers. Commander Hamilton's squadrons now knew they would go to Guadalcanal to operate with the Marines.

It was disappointing to the fighter pilots, who were aware that their F4Fs were now outclassed by a faster, more versatile aircraft in the form of Vought's F4U Corsair. The Marine fighter squadrons at Guadalcanal would fly Corsairs by the time VF-11 arrived because the "U-Bird" was considered unsuitable for carrier operations. The Wildcat was a well-proven aircraft, but now that the Sun Downers were to operate from a land base they would have preferred F4Us. The Grumman lacked not only the Corsair's speed, but its range, rate of climb and ammunition capacity. Furthermore, the F4F could be tricky as a gun platform - it tended to skid while firing.

One advantage was that there would probably be no shortage of Wildcats. Fighting Eleven and VF-21 were the last F4F squadrons engaged in prolonged combat, and the Fleet Aircraft Replacement Pool was well stocked with Wildcats from other units. As Ensign Vern Graham said, "We were concerned about being selected to 'use up' the remaining F4Fs . . . however, we were confident in it." Bill Leonard, as flight and operations officer, probably summed up the pilots' feelings when he said, "Committed to the F4F, we would not let our minds dwell too much on its deficiencies. VF-11 felt sensitive flying an obviously outdated machine but we were loyal to the F4F."

On April 25, 1943 Air Group 11 departed the Fijis for Guadalcanal. White took his Wildcats to Espiritu Santo that night and arrived at "The Canal" on Monday the 26th with thirty-four aircraft. Two had been delayed en route with mechanical problems but both shortly rejoined the squadron. White, Cady and Vogel each led one of VF-11's three elements to the destination with TBFs acting as navigation planes on the 600 mile flight. Fighting Eleven settled down at the Lunga Point strip better known as Fighter One, while Commander Hamilton's other three squadrons were based at nearby Henderson Field.

The ground echelon had previously arrived by ship or transport plane, and established a tent camp "in a delightful oasis of mud and mosquitoes in a coconut grove." The next day VF-11 was briefed by Col. Sam Moore, the colorful, swashbuckling Marine fighter commander. The Sun Downers were to fly under the tactical control of the Marine Corps, as the Leathernecks had been operating from the island for the past eight months. Later that morning, the 27th, VF-11's first patrol from "Cactus" was flown by Lieutenant Commander Vogel, Lieutenant (jg) Robert N. Flath, Lieutenant (jg) William R. Maxwell and Lieutenant (jg) Cyrus G. Cary. It was a local flight with nothing to report, but two days later Lieutenant Commander White led two divisions on an escort mission to Munda. The only enemy opposition was AA fire.

At the end of the first week—Sunday, May 2—VF-11 suffered its first loss. Sixteen Sun Downers escorting a strike to Munda were south of Vangunu at 14,000 feet when the exec, Sully Vogel, ran one of his fuel tanks dry and lost altitude while switching tanks. His element leader, Bob Maxwell, moved to port in order to regain sight of Vogel when the two Wildcats collided. Vogel's propeller sliced off the last six feet of Maxwell's fuselage.

Maxwell's F4F nosed up in a half-loop and fell into a flat spin. He managed to bail out and open his parachute but the other Wildcats had to continue the mission. At 1700 returning pilots spotted Maxwell in his life raft and reported his position, though by then it was too late to summon help. Vogel had aborted the mission, returning with a smashed canopy and rubber marks on one wing from Maxwell's tires.

"Maxie" was nowhere to be seen the next morning, nor anywhere for two weeks. A PBY brought him back to Guadalcanal on May 18 after a harrowing but safe sixteen days in enemy-occupied area. The intrepid South Carolinian had sailed his raft to Tetipari, arriving on the 5th. He walked the length of the island in seven days, encountering a crocodile which claimed dominion over a channel on a coral beach, but otherwise met no opposition. On the 13th he launched his raft for Rendova, where he knew he stood a chance of contacting an Australian Coast

Flying "no hands" in F4F No. 13, Charlie Wesley trimmed the plane and took this photo of the rest of his flight over the Solomons. Nearest Wildcat is No. 14 with a new off-color cowling; next is No. 21; furthest aircraft No. unknown. (C. Wesley)

Douglas "Dauntless" SBDs of VB-11 on a mission over the Solomons with VF-11 as escort. (J.S. Swope)

Watcher. He was met by friendly natives who took him to safety near Segi Lagoon on the 17th. Maxwell's fifth mission had been his last with VF-11, for he was flown to New Zealand where he spent two months in a hospital recuperating from his adventure.

Meanwhile, operations continued and despite lack of enemy aerial opposition, the losses also mounted. On May 6 during another strike against Munda, Ensign LeRoy Childs' aircraft dropped behind the formation, his engine smoking badly. The F4F splashed down north of the Rendova hook, and though Maxwell talked to natives who saw a parachute that day, only Childs' seat cushion was found.

Two days later three Sun Downers led by Lieutenant Lester Wall found enemy shipping in Blackett Strait. They blew a landing barge out of the water and then found a Japanese ship which was dead in the water. It turned out to be the **Oyashio**, a 2,400-ton destroyer of the **Kagero** class, which had struck a mine the previous night. The Wildcats raked the crippled ship repeatedly with .50 caliber fire, facilitating its eventual sinking five miles southwest of Rendova.

On May 26 the skipper himself achieved the dubious distinction of being the first VF-11 pilot to qualify for a Purple Heart. A 20 mm shell went through White's cockpit while he strafed Suavanau Point at Rekata Bay, causing a gash on his left hand. But he was on flight status again in a week.

Though things were slow in the air, the Squadron's living area was improved considerably by the industrious Sea Bees who built quonset huts and new shower stalls. Two pilots had been temporarily evacuated to New Zealand during the first couple of weeks, suffering from jaundice, but otherwise the squadron enjoyed largely good health. Dysentery was the most troublesome ailment but it grounded few pilots, and none for very long.

By the first week of June, VF-11 had been on Guadalcanal a month and a half, without a single claim for an enemy aircraft. The Sundowner appellation was beginning to seem unduly boastful, particularly in comparison to the achievements of the Marine squadrons. Gordon Cady's division finally broke the ice on June 7th when a thirty-two plane escort to Vila was abandoned due to weather. Cady had climbed his four planes to 10,000 feet and, seeing the route was clear farther west, received permission to continue.

The Wildcats were ten miles south of Segi when an estimated twenty-four Zeros were sighted approaching them overhead at 15,000 feet. At the same time Lieutenant (jg) Dan Hubler, the number four man, reported at least eight more directly above. Outnumbered eight to one and at a serious tactical disadvantage, Cady wisely decided to evade into clouds over Vangunu before it was too late.

But it was already too late for the other three. Hubler's plane was so badly shot up that he had to bail out, and even then the Japanese strafed him in the water. Fortunately all of them missed. Other Japanese fighters concentrated on Lieutenants (jg) Terry Holberton and Ed "Smiley" Johnson. Holberton recalls the encounter:

"Speculation had been that the Japanese used their machine guns with tracers to bore sight the target, then opened up with their 20 mm cannons. Some small shot came through the side of my aircraft, wiping out the circuit breakers and the instrument panel. All electricity went out, including the gun sight rings. I believe the shots were all from bullets. A larger shot hit me in the starboard wing root and took out the oil cooler. One of the smaller rounds ran down my arm from elbow to wrist, burning the skin.

"About that time I hit the cloud cover over Vangunu. I set the gyro compass to zero and made a sharp ninety degree turn to the left and counted slowly to thirty while on instruments. I reset the compass to zero again and turned 180 degrees, again counting slowly for thirty seconds, then turned left and came out of the clouds on the original course. There was Smiley just ahead of me chased by a Zero so intent on the kill that he never saw me.

"My windscreen was filled with the Zero so I didn't need sights. He was slightly above me and I pulled up and squeezed the trigger. Nothing happened because the electrical system was out. Then the engine quite due to the strain. I had no oil pressure and the prop was running wild. I pushed over to keep from stalling and headed for the vast lagoon between New Georgia and Vangunu.

"Dead sticking the plane into the water, I hit my head on the gun sight (still bear the scar between my eyebrows), and was knocked unconscious. The next thing I knew I was sitting in the cockpit with water up to my chin."

Smiley Johnson had little to smile about, as he was the only one left. Coaxing a damaged engine, he made a couple of inconclusive head-on passes at some

---

1. Maxwell returned to combat with a vengeance, flying with VF-4 off <u>Ranger</u> and VF-51 off <u>San Jacinto</u>, where he gained seven victories.

Zeros before he too bailed out. He landed in a clearing on Vangunu while the enemy pilots tried to kill him on the ground just as they tried to shoot Hubler in the water, with a similar lack of success.

Cady meanwhile had reached the clouds unharmed and dodged from cover to cover enroute to base. But he was twice presented with opportunities he couldn't resist, and thereby lived up to his formidable gunnery reputation. On both occasions when Cady emerged from a cloud to find a Zero in front of him, he shot them down. Then he raced back to Guadalcanal to help organize rescue efforts.

Amazingly, all three downed pilots returned safely, Hubler by native canoe the next day.

Bruised as he was, Holberton made for the nearest small island in his life raft, dressed his wounds and launched himself again toward the next island. After reaching shore and pulling his raft along the beach and through mangroves, he rested until dawn the following day. Continuing his shoreline trek, Holberton narrowly avoided an encounter with a crocodile, thereafter giving the fresh water mangroves a wide berth, and eventually came ashore near what seemed to be an abandoned native village. The following morning he heard voices and saw two silhouettes near a shack.

"I waited for a little light and entered the hut with my .45 drawn. The two men were natives, one old and one young. The young one dove out a window too quickly for me to shoot and hit the water below.

"I was yelling, 'American pilot! American pilot!', but the old man just kept cringing on the floor until I realized that he was looking down the barrel of my automatic and was scared to death. When the gun was lowered he called the young man, who came back. There was a lot of native chatter and sign language and I sat down to wait with the old man while the boy took off in a canoe."

No less than a chief returned with several other natives and an interpreter to bear Terry Holberton to another island. During the dangerous open water trek around New Georgia to Segi a flight of VF-11 Wildcats spotted the party and a J2F Duck flew to Segi to rescue Holberton.

But Smiley Johnson had an even more adventurous trek. Thinking he was on New Georgia, he nearly strolled into a Japanese camp and was almost seen by the enemy. He spent twelve days in a survival epic before finally locating friendly natives. Then with the help of an Australian coast watcher and natives he made it to Segi (on the Southern tip of New Georgia) and was retrieved, none the worse for wear, by a Navy Catalina. Stepping onto Henderson Field at Guadalcanal, on June 19th, Ed commented, "It looked as good as my own front yard in Coronado, except my wife was not there."

Later on the 7th, Ray Vogel led his division to Vila for some strafing and hedge-hopped the way home via New Georgia and Gatukai. But between Gatukai and the Russells, Vogel's wingman, Lieutenant (jg) Bob Flath, was bounced by two Zekes which badly shot up his plane. Vogel boresighted one Zero and shot it off Flath's tail and Flath dived for home. Vogel managed to elude the second bandit. In these first aerial encounters of June 7, VF-11 had come out even at three for three, but lost no pilots. However, it was painfully obvious that the Wildcats could not hope for much better than a draw when outnumbered and caught at a disadvantage.

The next combat came only five days later, with much better results. Four divisions under Bill Leonard were near the Russells returning to base from a long PBY escort when the fighter director reported a large bogey on radar at 0940. Leonard, Les Wall, Ken Viall and Charley Wesley reported their divisions available for interception and spent the next thirty-five minutes following radar vectors. Visual contact was made shortly after 1000 a little northwest of the Russells. Stacked from 23,000 to 26,000

Bill Leonard's F4F, No. 21 at fighter strip No. 2, Guadalcanal. (C. Barber)

Ensign Robert Flath in his Grumman F4F Wildcat on Guadalcanal. (R.N. Flath)

feet, the sixteen Wildcats saw some three dozen Zeros both above and below them. Leonard evaluated the situation, mainly concerned about the F4Fs' depleted fuel, as they had been in the air well over three hours. He radioed, "Make one pass and use remaining fuel to get home," which was seventy miles away

As was so often the case, it wasn't possible. Leonard exploded two Zekes, raising his career total to six, and then disengaged. But the Japanese pressed their numerical advantage and drew most of the other Wildcats into dogfights. Lieutenant (jg) Claude Ivie splashed a Zeke but was soon forced into a ditching near the Russells. The other pilots became scattered and fought singly or in pairs.

Leonard's second section didn't make it clear of the Zeros. Lieutenant (jg) Vern Graham and his wingman, Bob Gilbert, "became involved in assisting Marine F4Us who were severely outnumbered." as Graham put it. The Corsairs had been drawn to the combat and, with more fuel, stayed to fight.

Gilbert remained as long as he dared, claiming three kills, then broke off, rejoined Leonard and landed with less than four gallons of fuel. Lieutenant Ken Viall's division was bounced by several Zekes but Viall disregarded bandits on his tail and drew a bead on one of two Japanese dogging Lieutenant (jg) George Ricker's F4F. Viall fired and watched the Zero dive into the water. Les Wall's wingman Teddy Hull bagged two Zekes, one of which he literally shot out of Wall's sights. Then Wall was wounded by a 20 mm shell and ditched 100 yards offshore in the Russells. Lieutenant (jg) Lowell Slagle landed on the rough Russells strip, dangerously low on fuel.

But the standout performance was recorded by Bill Leonard's section leader, Vern Graham, who disregarded his fuel problem and stayed in the fight. Though it would by Graham's only combat in his thirty-three missions, it would make Sun Downer history.

"I was separated from Lieutenant Leonard on that first pass and from Gilbert very soon thereafter," Graham recalled. He dived on a Zeke slow-rolling behind an F4F and disintegrated it with a short burst. He set a second afire with a high side run and exploded a third head-on.

Graham now joined two Corsairs of VMF-121 and the mismatched trio attacked four Zekes and initiated an offensive weave. One F4U drew a Zeke straight across Graham's sights and his guns chopped large pieces from it. After that Graham had to give in to his rapidly diminishing fuel supply and he turned towards the Russells. But another Zeke appeared at his 12 o'clock high so he pulled up, fired, and saw it smoke and roll over. Then it was lost to sight. At this point Graham's engine quit and two more Zekes jumped his tail. The Marines were still on hand and shot down one, driving the other away.

Completely out of fuel, Graham describes his approach to the narrow landing strip cut into the coconut plantation on Russell Island:

"From some recess the motor drew a little more fuel. This helped me gain some speed and distance, which was fortunate, for without this added lift, I wouldn't have made it. Some of the other fellows weren't so fortunate.

"I didn't know that one of my wheels had been partly shot away and was no good for landing. When I saw I was going to make the strip, and let down the wheels and landing flaps, there was no indication that I was heading for trouble.

"As luck would have it, I struck a soft spot and the weakened wheel crumpled. My plane flipped over. [Bur. No. 03430. Sq. No. F-23]

"My head struck something and I knew no more until I awakened hours later in the hospital. They told me I had a fractured skull and a broken collar bone, but otherwise I was unhurt.

"The whole battle was hazy to me then, and I tried not to think about it. Some time later, Captain Ken Ford of VMF-121 came to see me. I didn't know him then. He said, 'Nice shooting, fellow. Thanks a lot.'

"I still didn't know what it was about. 'I was in the F4U you helped out in that scrap,' he said. ' The one with a Jap on its tail.'

"I nodded vaguely. 'What happened to the Jap?' I asked.

Charles Wesley in F4F No. 13 on Guadalcanal. (C.Wesley)

Plane Captain N.R. Donaldson poses with "his" Wildcat. (C. Wesley)

"'What happened to him? Why, you got him. Didn't you know?'"

Ace in a day, Vern Graham was awarded the Navy Cross and sent home to recover from his injuries.[1]

The Sun Downers could now justifiably claim their self-appointed title. In this action they were credited with fourteen Zekes for four F4Fs (including Graham's) and no pilots. It looked like a hard record to beat, but in merely four days VF-11 would have another chance.

At 1230 on June 16 Marine fighter command alerted VF-11 of a very large incoming Japanese formation. Between 1310 and 1340 the Sun Downers scrambled seven divisions - twenty-eight Wildcats - which dispersed to meet the estimated 120 bandits. Actually there were twenty-four Val dive bombers escorted by seventy Zekes, their obvious target being the crowded American shipping around Tulagi. Sully Vogel, Ken Viall, Walt Hiebert and Charley Wesley's divisions went to orbit Cape Esperance while Frank Quady and John Ramsey's divisions took station over the ships in the bay. Lieutenant Commander White set up over Henderson Field with his four planes.

By swinging wide to the southwest the Japanese eluded early interception from the Russells and were reported only twenty-five miles south of Fighter One at 1400, heading northeast. Frank Quady sighted the dive bombers with Zekes deployed on either flank at 15,000 feet and led Henry White, Homer "Red" Schild and John Cooke out of the sun in high overhead and stern runs. Quady recounts the action:

"We were at 25,000 feet and the enemy consisted of two shallow vees of nine or ten dive bombers each, with a column of Zeros slightly above and on either side. There were twenty-five to thirty Zeros, and I made a stern run into the leading vee of bombers, shooting at the second plane from the right end. The dive bomber began to smoke and fell off to the right. Meanwhile, the end plane pulled up to avoid the damaged Val and I gave him a burst. He immediately shuddered, smoked and followed his companion down.

"I then pulled up and around and commenced to head-on with a Zero. I emptied the rest of my ammunition into him and he smoked and fell downward.

"I received three 20 mm cannon shots and numerous 7.7s and spun down. With a Zero following, I went into a cloud where I stayed until the field was clear. There was a Mitsubishi twin-engine bomber also flying around in the cloud and I tried to give him a burst, but my ammunition was exhausted. My controls were all but shot away and I thought of bailing out but finally made the field."

Lieutenant (jg) Henry "Sol" White related his version of the engagement:

"I peeled off after Lieutenant Quady and opened up on the Val on the inside of the formation. My burst hit him in the right wing which sheared off. He went straight into the mountain on the right.

"I then put about 100 rounds into the third plane from the end, breaking off when he began to emit heavy smoke and fall off to the right."

Lieutenant (jg) John Ramsey, approaching the Japanese from the northwest with a considerable altitude advantage, exploited it fully.

" I had taken a division which included one pilot on the sick list, another pilot who had been on the ground for three weeks awaiting transfer, and a third who had been shot down nine days previously and had been back with the Squadron less than a week.

"All I could see around me were Zeros and three F4Fs. Several Zeros made passes at

1. From a story in *True* magazine, 1944.

Lieutenant (j.g.) George Ricker (above) and Lieutenant (j.g.) Teddy Hull (below) were killed in action on June 16, 1943. (R.N. Flath)

me and one made a beautiful overhead run. I gave him a burst and he broke into flames and fell.

"I looked around to find almost in formation with me, a cream-colored dive bomber with black markings burning merrily, with a Wildcat on his tail. I saw two more of the same type. My motor was smoking and oil was being splattered over the windshield, but I managed to give the second one a burst and he burned.

"I was wondering whether to bail out, but the Zeros around and the anti-aircraft bursts dissuaded me from jumping, and I came in making a dead-stick landing."

Lieutenant (jg) John Pressler splashed two Zekes but then himself landed in the water with sudden engine stoppage.

Lieutenant Commander White contacted the dive bombers just as they pushed over on the ships 15,000 feet below. White and his wingman, Lieutenant (jg) Teddy Hull, started on the Vals in line astern and White hit two which fell away smoking, claimed as probables. After a brief tussle with a Zeke, White looked around and Hull was nowhere in sight.

But White's second section had a field day. Charlie Stimpson and Jim Swope made repeated runs on the diving Vals and did nearly as well as Vern Graham had in his combat four days before. Skull Stimpson splashed four dive bombers and Swope bagged three; the first time either of them had scored.

By now the dive-bombing attack was over. Two U.S. ships had been hit by bombs and the Vals were fleeing north at low level. Vogel's sixteen Wildcats slammed into the combat over the Savo-Tulagi-Lunga area and the sky was immediately filled with dogfights from 20,000 feet on down. [1]Lieutenant Ken Viall knocked two Vals into the water and then got a Zeke. Lieutenant (jg) William J. Masoner claimed two Zekes while George Ricker pursued one with Chandler Boswell low on the deck. But the two F4Fs collided and hit the water. Both pilots were lost.

Then it was over. Army, Navy and Marine fighters wheeled around, temporarily alerted by a false alarm of more bogies, and began landing at Henderson Field and the two fighter strips. It was thought that ninety-four of the estimated 120 enemy aircraft had been shot down, with VF-11 claiming thirty-one, the largest share of the kills. Since it is known the Japanese dispatched exactly ninety-four planes, some overclaiming evidently resulted, but not very much. Admiral Samuel Eliot Morison relates that the

1. **The only loss was USS Celano, AK76.**

June 16, 1943, just after a dogfight. Jim Swope examines Zero cannon shell damage to his left wing. Charles Stimpson is on his right. (C. Wesley)

Charlie Stimpson in his Wildcat, No. F4, Bureau No. 12163, after downing four Val dive bombers on 16 June 1943. (Mrs. M.B. Stimpson)

enemy formation was almost completely annihilated, losing the equivalent of almost two carrier air groups.

In return for thirty-one kills by seventeen of the twenty-eight Sun Downers flying the mission, four Wildcats and three pilots were gone. It was another indication of VF-11's major role in the battle, as only two other U.S. fighters had been lost. John Pressler made it safely to shore from his ditched F4F, and Army pilots reported a P-40 colliding with a Wildcat, almost certainly White's wingman, Teddy Hull. Apparently none of the three missing Sun Downers fell to enemy aircraft; collision was the often unavoidable result of so many planes crowded into such a limited airspace.

Rear Admiral Marc Mitscher, Commander Air Forces Solomons, was so appreciative of VF-11's contribution to the record victory that he sent two cases of whiskey by way of congratulation. The Sun Downers employed Mitscher's gift to convince two war correspondents that VF-11 was the only outfit on Guadalcanal worth writing about.

A single kill was registered on June 21 when Lieutenant (jg) Homer Schild of Frank Quady's division

1. Morison, S.E. <u>History of U.S. Naval Operations in WW II</u>, Vol 6., Page 140.

Charlie Stimpson's Wildcat, No. 4, and Engineering Chief, Petty Officer L.M. Huckabay. Note wing drop tank. (Mrs. M.B. Stimpson)

found a Nell bomber near Santa Isabel. Separated from the others, Schild made three passes and shot the bomber down for his third victory. But VF-11 lost another aircraft when Lieutenant (jg) Henry White, the colorful West Virginian, overshot the runway while making a forced landing and nosed into the Tenaru River. Long flying hours, heavy combat and general fatigue were taking their

Lieutenant (j.g.) Henry "Sol" White ended up in Guadalcanal's Tenaru River on June 21, 1943 when making a forced landing with a damaged plane. The Wildcat was a washout but White escaped serious injury. (Tim Enander)

toll. Despite the fact that VF-11's excellent mechanics had actually presented the pilots with a "new" Wildcat built out of spares, both aircraft and pilot availability declined. Dan Hubbard wiped out an F4F in a landing accident, damaging three others, and was evacuated with injuries.

Admiral Mitscher said VF-11 was due for rotation, but not immediately. On July 6 the Sun Downers escorted TBFs to Kula Gulf and a division composed of Charley Wesley, Chester Parker, Charlie Stimpson and Jim Swope tangled with six or eight Zekes. The Japanese pilots must have had a grudge against Texans, for they all tied on to Swope's tail. Stimpson destroyed one from directly astern while Wesley and Parker made overhead runs on the others as Swope engaged in violent aerobatics. A superior airman, Swope shook the Zekes after Wesley and Parker each splashed one. Jim then bagged a Zeke but his Wildcat was so badly shot up that he could only fly it back to the junk heap.

Fighting Eleven's last combat at Guadalcanal occurred three days later, July 9, 1943 when Lieutenant Commanders White and Vogel led two divisions on CAP over Rendova. An estimated forty to fifty Zekes in two waves were reported, but Bob Flath developed a rough engine just then so Bill Masoner was ordered to escort him home. In the dogfight which followed, Skull Stimpson

Sun Downer pilots pose behind their score board on June 17, 1943. (L. to R.) Back two rows: Parker, Holberton, Ogilvie, Flath, Ivie, Gaston, Work, Martin, Cooke, Stimpson, Swope, Masoner, Hubler, Hubbard. Second row: Hiebert, Leonard, Wall, Cady (behind left prop), C.M. White, CO, Vogel, (Exec), Quady, Pressler (to the right of the right prop), Pimentel, Johnson and Vaill. Bottom row, kneeling: Cary, Gilbert, Schild, Wesley, Ramsey, H.S. White, Coppola, Jones. Not shown: Dayhoff, Graber, Graham, Slagle, all of whom had been evacuated for jaundice or wounds. (C.Wesley)

Lieutenant (j.g.) Cyrus George Cary was lost during operations on July 9, 1943. (R.N. Flath)

repeated his performance of the sixth by shooting a Zeke off Jim Swope, who shortly splashed one himself for his fifth victory. Vern Gaston and Clarence White teamed up to destroy a third Zeke, but it wasn't one-sided. During the hassle, White glimpsed an F4F in a vertical dive off Rendova. It was Cy Carey, Vogel's wingman, who failed to return. Vogel was also hit, taking three 20 mm shells in one wing.

The Sun Downers continued the strenuous Rendova CAPs through July 11th. These missions averaged over three and one-half hours each, and some pilots (Bill Leonard, for example) flew two sorties some days, logging as much as eight hours, much of it on oxygen. Finally, on the twelfth, launching for the last time from Fighter One, VF-11 began a deployment south from Cactus, homeward bound.

In eleven weeks the Squadron had been credited with fifty-five enemy aircraft: thirty-seven Zekes, seventeen Vals and one Nell. Five pilots had been killed in action but only Carey was actually lost to enemy aircraft. Three other pilots - Maxwell, Graham and Hubbard - were evacuated with injuries. Twelve Wildcats had been lost in aerial combat, for a kill-loss ratio of four and one-half to one. Probably another half-dozen F4Fs were destroyed or wrecked in accidents and a couple of others were written off with extensive battle damage.

In their first tour the Sun Downers had produced four aces: Stimpson and Leonard with six kills, Graham and Swope with five each. Graham may have identified the source of VF-11's success when he said, "Many times I was grateful for the opportunity of flying with so many well-trained, talented Regular Navy men." Fenton, White, Cady and the others had done their jobs well; the results proved it.

During a two-week stop at Espiritu Santo, the pilots encountered the airplane most of them yearned for, the brand-new F6F-3 Hellcat. Bill Leonard and some others were anxious to try out the new Grummans, which

Bob Flath (left) and Terry Holberton were two of several awarded Purple Hearts for wounds received during the Guadalcanal tour. (R.N. Flath)

were being accumulated for VF-12. "The F6F-3 was almost as good as the F4U in fighter performance and alleged to be as good as the F4F in carrier behavior," Leonard recalled. After flying the Hellcat, Leonard and some others hoped to take them to Guadalcanal for introduction to combat.

But it wasn't to be. The Squadron went aboard the escort carrier **Chanango** in early August and arrived at NAS Alameda on the 21st. Many of the pilots were dispersed and assigned to other duties. Quady and Leonard, who had completed their second tours, went to Admiral Mitscher's staff at ComAirWestCoast. Clarence White joined the staff of ComAirPac while Vogel returned to Annapolis for medical treatment and duty at the Naval Academy. Gordon Cady was promoted to Lieutenant Commander and took over as C.O. of VF-11, effective September 25, 1943.

FAR WESTERN PACIFIC

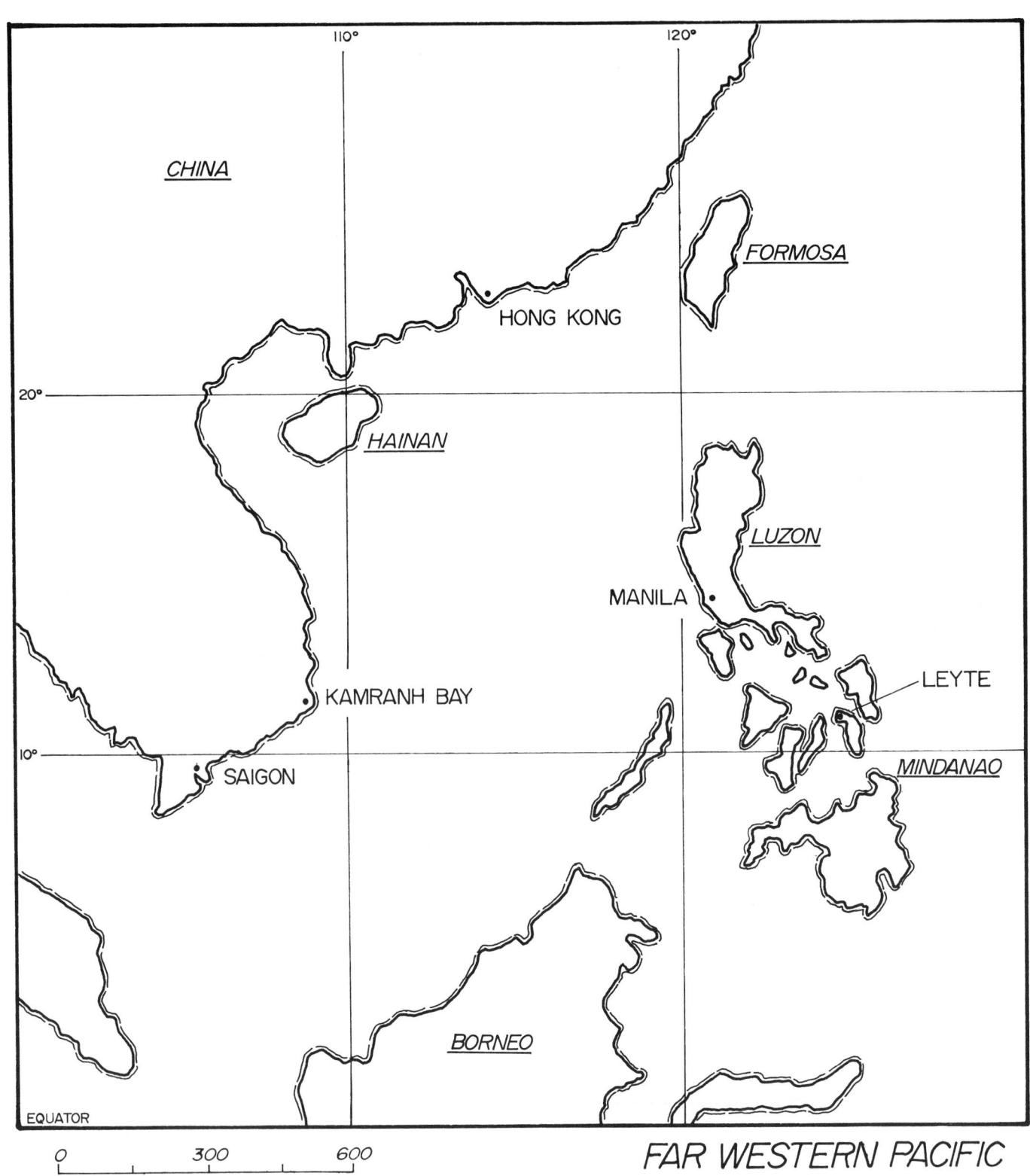

SECOND TOUR OF COMBAT

The Sun Downers began a training and reforming cycle with a nucleus of veterans such as Stimpson, Swope, Henry White, John Ramsey and a few others. At the same time a number of SBD pilots who had flown with Bombing 11 and Scouting 11 at Guadalcanal transferred into Cady's unit. One of these was Lieutenant (jg) Bob Saggau, an All-American halfback on the 1938-40 Notre Dame football team. Saggau and the other dive bomber pilots simply decided they wanted a chance to fly fighters and "It was actually very simple," he recalled. "We requested through channels to transfer to VF-11 and were so authorized."

Another pilot with a harder time getting transferred in was the new exec, Lieutenant Eugene G. Fairfax. A determined, aggressive twenty-seven year old, Fairfax had enlisted in the Navy in 1934. He entered Annapolis in 1935, eventually became captain of the boxing team, and graduated in 1939. First assigned to battleships, he transferred to aviation and received his wings in March, 1942. Fairfax flew OS2U float planes from **USS Tennessee** but soon tired of the rather tame life of an observation pilot and, in the words of the fleet air personnel officer, "stuck out his neck about forty feet" by going out of channels to request a transfer to fighters.

The request was granted and Gene Fairfax joined VF-11 in September, 1943. But though he arrived with 675 hours in his logbook, his work was cut out for him. The phrase "arrogant fighter pilots" has been overworked, but some Sun Downers' initial reaction to receiving an OS2U pilot as exec was less than enthusiastic. However, Gordon Cady was on top of the situation. He had Jim Swope introduce Fairfax to fighters, and before long the new exec was accepted by the old hands.

Many of the middle-grade pilots came from instructing duties, such as Lieutenant (jg) Jimmie E. Savage, the easygoing Texan destined to become the Sun Downers' number three ace. Cady gave Jim Swope his pick of the young ensigns for a wingman and Swope selected H.B. Moranville, a twenty-year-old Nebraskan who had quit college when the flying bug bit. But the new pilots weren't all reservists. Lieutenant Robert E. Clements, the flight officer, had been a year behind Fairfax at Annapolis and was six months out of Pensacola. Originally assigned to SBDs, Clements had gone to Bill Leonard at San Diego to arrange a transfer to VF-11. The squadron trained on F4F-4s until early October when F6F-3s became available.

Not long after acquiring Hellcats the Sun Downers also acquired a mascot. All pilots had to qualify on the pistol range, and the range instructor gave Gordon Cady one of a litter of Boston bull terrier pups. The dog was christened Gunner and Cady delegated Blake Moranville, then the youngest pilot in the squadron, to be its official caretaker. Blake and Gunner were soon inseparable.

In January 1944 VF-11 moved briefly to Crow's Landing for night flying, then back to Alameda in February for initial carrier qualifications aboard the escort carrier **Copahee**, where Gunner first tried out his sea legs. Finally, in late March, the reorganized Air Group 11 deployed to Hawaii, with aircraft, aboard the new fleet

F6F-5 Hellcats of VF-11 are armed with rockets for a practice mission from Hilo, Hawaii. (E.G. Fairfax)

All officers and enlisted men of VF-11 at Hilo, Hawaii. (L to R - Sitting) Enlisted Men: Rouse, Eaton, Donaldson, Hampton, Saville, Click, Theimer, Berry, Manthey, Watson, Reich, Butterly, Clayton, Bell, Brouillard, Edwards. Officers: (Row 1) Hardy (standing), Seated: Dayhoff (KIA), Flath, Holberton, Ramsey, Savage, Crusoe, Fairfax, Cady (KOA), Clements, Meyers, Griffin, Lee (KOA), Swope, Marin, Parsley. (Row 2) Lloyd, Brateres (KOA), Goldberg (KIA), MacBride, Morris, White, Cyr, Stimpson, Saggau, Dance (KIA), Coeur, Hintze, Zink, James, Moranville, Boring. Rear Row: Smith, Warren, Willis, Chase (KIA), Robcke, Sims (KIA), Ptacek (KIA), Nellis, Meade, Suddreth, Farley, Williams, Blair (KIA), Parsons, Lizotte, Zoecklein, and DeRolf (KIA). (G. Theimer)

carrier **Wasp**. Fighting 11 went ashore where Cady soon initiated an intensive training program. In order to obtain maximum experience from each flight, three divisions took off before dawn on most days for an average duration of three hours. This provided training in night flying and navigation. One division acted as bombers while the other two practiced escort technique based on Cady's "roving weave."

The twelve Hellcats practiced air-to-air and air-to-ground gunnery at the firing range before turning for home. But an added touch of realism was added whenever a radar director could vector the Sun Downers onto a formation of Army fighters, most often Seventh Air Force P-47s. The Hellcats usually had the best of these mock combats, for an F6F could nearly always turn inside a Thunderbolt, though the "Jugs" were noticeably faster. Other practice missions included a few "group gropes" with VB-11's SB2Cs and VT-11's TBMs.

Subsequent moves were made to Maui and Hilo with more carrier landings in July on the escort carrier **Kadashan Bay**. The Air Group was in Hawaii for five months, which to some eager youngsters like Blake "Rabbit" Moranville seemed "like forever." But the time was made immensely more pleasant as the Sun Downers renewed their friendship with the Von Tempskys. The first-tour pilots were naturally well acquainted with the family, and the new pilots soon felt at home on the sprawling estate. So much so, in fact, that three Sun Downers were constantly at the plantation, rotating every two days when the relief arrived in three F6Fs. Cady and the crew presented Alexa with a four-star flag symbolic of her position as "ComWolfPack" and whenever the ensign was flown it was interpreted as the all-clear signal for arriving pilots to indulge in a spectacular buzz job. If the flag was not visible, it meant that potentially unappreciative visitors were aboard and the pilots were to conduct themselves as Congress intended for officers and gentlemen.

In mid-August Gordon Cady was relieved as C.O. and ordered to Admiral John McCain's staff with Task Force 38 as operations officer. Gene Fairfax, now a lieutenant commander, took over and Bob Clements became executive officer. They only had about three weeks to settle into their new jobs before shipping out, for the Air Group had orders for the Western Pacific. A final few deck landings were made aboard **Ranger** in the first few days of September, by which time most of the Hellcat pilots had about 300 hours logged in F6Fs. The more senior pilots had from 900 to 1200 hours total time.

But the squadron was divided for the trip west. The maintenance personnel, minus aircraft, boarded **Wasp** while most officers were delegated the entirely unwelcome chore of serving as armed guards on a transport ship loaded with former prisoners from the Navy prison at Treasure Island. Air Group 11 under Commander Fred R. Schrader was reunited at Manus Harbor in the Admiralties during mid-September. Gene Fairfax had forty-five pilots under him, young men from thirty-three of the forty-eight states whose ages ranged from nineteen to twenty-eight.

The Hornet, CV-12, an Essex class aircraft carrier. (National Archives via U.S. Naval Institute.)

Seven Sun Downers remained from the Guadalcanal tour: Nelson Dayhoff, Bob "Cac" Flath, John Ramsey, Charlie Stimpson, Jim Swope, Henry White, and Dan Work. Schrader's squadrons were to replace Air Group 2 aboard **USS Hornet** (CV-12) and received most of their initial aircraft from the veteran unit. Fighting 11 inherited VF-2's Hellcats, a mixture of F6F-3s and -5s, all sporting the white ball on the tail. For this reason, Air Group 11 retained identical markings to Air Group 2. A night-fighter detachment flying radar-equipped Hellcats was permanently assigned to **Hornet**, but would share some of VF-11's facilities once aboard ship.

Hornet's skipper, Captain A.K. "Artie" Doyle, welcomed the new fliers aboard and used the time available to exercise the air group in a shakedown cruise. Meanwhile, Gordon Cady had been conscientiously working on an operations plan for the Fast Carrier Task Force and, though fatigued from long hours, flew from carrier to carrier putting his customary personal touch on the preparations. While landing aboard **Wasp** his arresting hook broke and his aircraft slammed inverted into the barrier. Cady died in the crash, a serious blow to the Sun Downers' morale. He was replaced as task force operations officer by his friend, Bill Leonard.

Task Force 38 sortied from Manus in early October, taking Air Group 11 back into the war for a second time. But it was over a week to the operations area and there were other distractions. On the fourth, Lieutenant J.S. Brown of VF-11 made the 10,000th landing on **Hornet** and Captain Doyle presented the Sun Downers with a cake to mark the occasion. The next day Ensign S.J. Richardson was forced to ditch with a broken oil line. He suffered a slight cut on the head but was rescued by a destroyer.

On October 9, 1944 Gene Fairfax counted forty-six Hellcats available for operations. He was going to need them, because the next day would be VF-11's first combat mission from **Hornet.**

The target was Japanese shipping in the Nansei Shoto group between Okinawa and Japan. The fourth fighter mission of the day, October 10, demonstrated VF-11's proficiency even though nearly all the pilots were new to combat. The Sun Downers averaged nineteen seconds between each launch, only one-quarter second short of the record. Armed with bombs and rockets, the F6Fs went low over Miyako Jima's anchorage to get at enemy shipping. Lieutenant J.E. " Doc" Savage took his division down on a 5,500-ton transport, pressing through AA fire to skip-bomb the vessel. Ensign Ken Chase, the baby of the squadron, got a direct hit with his 500-pound bomb but was almost immediately shot off Savage's wing and crashed in the water. Lieutenant John Ramsey and Lieutenant (jg) W.H. Boring rocketed a destroyer tender which beached itself and burned. The Sun Downers had probably sunk two ships, though Chase was lost. During the day Ensign George Lindesmith evened the score when he caught a Val dive bomber and shot it down, the first kill of the tour.

Operations continued the next day, and this time VF-11 proved the near-record launch of the 10th was no fluke. Thirty-one Hellcats and three SB2Cs were launched with an average seventeen and one-half seconds separation. The teletype in the ready room clacked out a message, "The boys set a new record on that launch . . . The captain is tickled."

On October 12 the Fast Carrier Task Force went to work farther south, launching strikes against Formosa.

Pilot briefing aboard <u>Hornet</u>. Jimmie "Doc" Savage is at far left front, and Bill Eccles sits with mascot. (J.S. Swope)

The first fighter mission of the day launched at 0545 for Takao and Hieto. The Sun Downers damaged some shipping but were mostly concerned with shooting up airfields. Ensign Lindesmith, who had notched the first aerial victory of the cruise only two days before, was last seen strafing Hieto Airfield. Lieutenant Commander Bob Clements, the executive officer, notched the second kill by downing an Oscar. Lieutenant G.L. Morris was the only other pilot to engage, claiming a Tony probably shot down.

The next day was Friday the 13th, and it was no joke. It started badly when one of **Hornet's** night fighter Hellcats landed with guns charged, and the bump set off several rounds. Another night fighter and some SB2Cs were damaged.

Strike 1-C launched shortly before 1300 against Takao City, led by the CAG, Commander Schrader. Doc Savage described the attack from his perspective:

"My division and Lieutenant Nelson W. Dayhoff's division took off from the **USS Hornet** thirty minutes before dawn and formed with two other divisions of fighters from the **USS Wasp** (VF-14). We proceeded toward Formosa, some 175 miles away, setting our course for Hieto Airfield, at 15,000 feet. Our primary mission was to shoot down airborne aircraft; secondary mission was to destroy planes on the ground.

"Things were uneventful until we crossed the range of mountains on the extreme eastern side of the Island. Hieto lay just other other side of these mountains and we had hardly passed over the top when the AA started. We flew around awhile, weaving back and forth by divisions, looking for airborne opposition. None could be found, so I took my divisions down to strafe.

"Hieto was one of the major airfields on Formosa and served as a staging field for the Philippines, so ground targets were plentiful there. The AA was heavy so we dove by divisions at a fifty-five degree angle using full throttle from 12,000 and leveling off by 1,000 feet. I noticed two Jap planes milling around above us, dropping phosphorous bombs at our formation just before each strafing run. On our sixth pass they came down after my division - one of them made a run on me, but overshot as I cut my throttle completely. He had so much speed from diving that he couldn't stay behind me. As he shot by I added full throttle and dove with him as he split s'ed to the deck. He leveled off at 500 feet and I closed to 800 feet and fired my six 50 calibers from dead astern. He started a roll, but flamed while on his back and dove straight for the ground burning, and exploded upon hitting the deck.

"I formed my division quickly and sent one section home, as the section leader had been hit by AA on the last strafing run. I took some pictures of the nine burning planes on the field, as I had a photo plane that morning.

Lieutenant Jimmie "Doc" Savage. (B. Tillman)

"I left Hieto then and proceeded north to Okoyama Airfield, which is used for staging aircraft also, and was the largest and most important plane assembly plant and field on Formosa. B-29s from China had made one night raid on this field once before, so the Japs had AA guns everywhere around this area. I had Lieutenant Dayhoff's division cover me while I took photographs with my oblique camera at 1,500 feet. He stayed at 8,000 feet, drawing part of the AA fire. After getting the required pictures, we started strafing ground targets and fired seven transport planes before my wingman was hit by AA.

"We immediately formed the three remaining divisions and headed for home; I wanted to get my pictures back as the B-29s from China were scheduled for another night raid and would need the information. We landed aboard the **Hornet** at 0930."

The otherwise successful strike was marred by the loss of Commander Schrader whose Hellcat was hit by AA and splashed while strafing a seaplane base. Late that evening Ensign Leon Lee ditched, out of fuel, in **Hornet's** landing pattern. He could not be located in the dark and a daylight search proved fruitless.

Jim Swope and Hellcat prepare to launch from Hornet, October, 1944. (National Archives via Charles Graham.)

October 14th would be one of the Sun Downers' best days, but it was also the worst. Five fighter pilots were lost, the first at 0430 when Lieutenant Ed Helgerson's F6F-5N taxied off the flight deck in the dark. The early sweep found airborne targets and three pilots scored singles - two Judys and a Tony - while Lieutenant Morris repeated his score of the twelfth with a probable Tony. But Ensign Henry Ptacek was last seen in combat with a Tony and failed to return.

The main encounter of the day resulted when seven Hellcats under "Nellie" Dayhoff and Doc Savage were vectored onto a large enemy formation approaching the task group at 1420. Savage describes the action:

"Enemy planes had kept us up at General Quarters all night. None of us slept. Next morning found my and Lieutenant Dayhoff's divisions in the ready room in 'conditions eleven' (airborne in ten minutes). Around noon we were scrambled, and sent to 20,000 feet by the fighter director. I immediately received a vectors off, 275 degrees, bogey 12 o'clock, eighty miles'.

"After several minutes the fighter director said, 'Vectors port 265 degrees, bogey one o'clock, angles 18,000 feet, fifty miles'. After flying about fifty miles from the task force, I tally-hoed many bogies two o'clock up, fifteen miles. Fighter director said, 'Attack and good luck.'

"I counted thirty-four planes and called back for help, climbing for altitude. We made our initial attack out of the sun with about a 1,000 foot advantage. Lieutenant Charles Stimpson was leading Lieutenant Dayhoff's division as Dayhoff's radio wasn't working. He went after the dive bombers with his division and I took the fighters just astern of the bombers. Stimpson flamed three bombers before they knew we were there. I closed on two Zekes and flamed them.

"I moved to the left on another section, when I saw tracers come by my wing. I turned very steeply, but the Jap had the advantage and I couldn't out-turn him but he couldn't hit me, because he couldn't get enough lead on me. After several turns, Lieutenant Stimpson saw him and came over and shot the Jap down. I dove on two more Jap fighters but missed and overshot. I came back but they had gone, so I climbed for more altitude. I looked down and noticed several planes going down in flames. I turned left and saw two more planes closing in on me from astern. They split and I was boxed with one on either side. I turned right but the one on the left immediately started hitting me. One 12.7 shattered the instrument panel and I split S'ed, rolling to the right going straight down at full throttle. I dove from 15,000 feet to 500 feet and pulled out and noticed streamers coming off my wings, but the Japs were still after me. I headed for some clouds some fifteen miles away and at approximately 5,000 feet I managed to gain distance on the Japs by using full power and was able to gain altitude at a very slow rate, otherwise I'd lose too much speed in climbing.

"I reached the clouds and got in them OK, but wasn't in the cloud bank very long before I was in real trouble, as my instruments weren't working. The needle and ball was shot away and I had tumbled my Gyro-Horizon when I split S'ed and rolled on the way down from high altitude. After a while I got into a spin, but recovered by sheer luck as I kicked the rudder against the way I thought I was spinning and sure enough that was right."

After the initial attack in which Charlie Stimpson had downed three Zekes and his wingman, Ensign Fred Blair another, both formations had been broken.

Stimpson and Blair now scissored on each other and Skull got a good burst into another Tony close behind his wingman but like the first one, it only smoked and fell away. Blair returned the favor by flaming a Zeke which was behind his leader. Reversing his turn, Stimpson saw another Zeke firing at Blair, hitting him badly. Stimpson fired at wide deflection and blew one wing off the Zeke, his fifth certain kill of the combat.

"Blair had been hit and I saw his belly tank on fire," Stimpson said. "I told him to drop it and dive for the deck. I crossed over him but only one Zeke attempted to follow and he scared off when I fired my remaining ammunition in front of him." Stimpson then watched his wingman ditch the crippled Hellcat, which sank quickly in the rough sea. Fred Blair did not get out.

Back aboard **Hornet** noses were counted and the hassle was evaluated. Three other pilots were missing. Lieutenant (jg) Sam Goldberg was never seen after the fight began and his wingman Ensign Lepianka, wounded in one shoulder, flopped down on the deck without flaps or wheels. "Nellie" Dayhoff, one of the veterans of the Guadalcanal tour, was also missing. His number two, Lieutenant (jg) J.A. Zink, reported that both had splashed Judys on the first pass but then were jumped from above by Zekes. Dayhoff killed one of them and Zink torched another Judy. Then a Zeke hit Dayhoff from overhead and Zink followed his leader all the way down to the water, watching him crash.

Doc Savage returned later than the others, but only barely as he recalled:

"I came out of the cloud bank headed straight down but straightened out by 3,000 feet and looked around to get my bearings. My electric compass was out as was my radio. I knew the Japs had chased me almost due west for some twenty-five miles and that I intercepted them some sixty miles out on a heading of 275 and 265 degrees, so I looked at the sun and flew the opposite direction, being careful to conserve fuel. I flew this course for an hour having no success. I started an expanding square search and forty-five minutes later I spotted a destroyer. I identified myself as friendly and flew by the bridge at slow speed telling them I was lost by the visual signal. Several minutes later a flight of Hellcats arrived and took me home. The destroyer had radioed the **Hornet** that I was out there lost and she had set her CAP out to pick me up. I landed aboard, having been given up for lost after being two hours overdue and reported 'probably shot down'. The fellows gave me a royal welcome. I was so happy to get home I just couldn't hold back the tears. I think all hands understood how I felt."

The final verdict on the combat of October 14th was fourteen definite kills and two probables for the loss of three pilots and four aircraft. Later during the day Ensigns Jake Robcke and George Anderson both splashed Frances snoopers near the task force. Fighting 11 had shot down at least nineteen enemy aircraft on October 14. Three Judys were added the next day but Ensign Robert C. Dance, who got one Judy, was shot down in the dogfight which followed. He bailed out, but that was the last seen of him. Another F6F was lost when Ensign Jacobsen hit **Hornet's** island in a landing accident, but the pilot escaped serious injury.

On the 16th four divisions on CAP engaged Tojos and Oscars, and came out nicely on top twelve to nothing. John Ramsey splashed two Tojos while Jim Swope, also breaking into the scoring column again, got a confirmed and a probable, as did Lieutenant (jg) Clyde Parsley. Swope's element leader, "Rabbit" Moranville, made his first kill by downing one of the four Oscars claimed. Lieutenant Henry White claimed the only Zeke of the day, joining Stimpson, Swope and Ramsey as the only Sun Downers to score on both tours.

Jim Swope appears as he would be equipped in flight at high altitude. (J.S. Swope)

Sun Downer pilots manning their Hellcats on <u>Hornet</u>. (H.B. Moranville)

By October 18th the fast carriers were launching against Manila in support of the Philippines invasion, and VF-11 cut down nine more bandits. Bob Clements raised his score to three with a Tojo and an Oscar but Lieutenant Dick Cyr, a former SBD pilot, was bell of the brawl. It seemed he outshot both Vern Graham and Charlie Stimpson for the Squadron's one-day record when he returned with claims for six Oscars. But subsequent evaluation reduced the figure to four confirmed and two probables. It was a heart-breaker, for Cyr never had another opportunity to score.* Ensign Warren DeRolf failed to return, and was last seen near Manila. Then during recovery of the evening CAP George Anderson's F6F splashed into the water, probably from heavy battle damage. He was the eleventh pilot lost in nine days.

By now the **Hornet** had a new air group commander, thirty-two-year-old Commander R.E. Riera. A veteran aviator, Emmett Riera was an Annapolis grad and "kissing cousin" of Gene Fairfax's wife, Juliana. He already had won a Navy Cross as C.O. of Bombing Squadron 20 but flew only one mission as CAG-11 in an accustomed SB2C before gaining approval from Captain Doyle to check out in an F6F while still at sea. From then on he flew regularly with VF-11, leading his own division.

The task group was near Yap enroute to the fleet anchorage at Ulithi on October 24 when word was received that major elements of the Imperial Japanese Navy were in Philippine waters. **Hornet** immediately put about and hurried back west. Air Group 11 missed all of the intense action of the 24th in the Battle of Leyte Gulf, but at 1030 on the 25th, sixteen Hellcats and twelve Helldivers were launched 350 nautical miles east of the enemy's reported position. It was one of the longest strike missions of the war, but every air group was needed to take advantage of this final opportunity.

The Japanese force off Samar was one of three which approached Leyte Gulf from the west. Admiral Jizaburo Ozawa's carrier force well to the north was a decoy to draw U.S. carriers away from San Bernardino Strait, where Admiral Kurita's powerful surface force hoped to trap American shipping. The Japanese southern group had been severely defeated in Suriagao Strait during the night of the 24-25th.

Originally composed of five battleships, thirteen cruisers and fifteen destroyers, Kurita's center force had been reduced to four battlewagons, four cruisers and seven destroyers by the morning of the 25th. The **Intrepid** and **Cabot** air groups had already arrived when the **Hornet** strike sighted the still-formidable armada. Commander Smith of VB-11, the strike leader, ordered VF-11 down to suppress AA fire while the SB2Cs prepared to attack. The Sun Downers pressed through spectacular flak, making repeated runs, only to be bitterly frustrated by negligible results. Few bomb hits were made, and TBMs from other air groups suffered extremely poor torpedo performance. Some Sun Downers reported that "tin fish" turned as much as 90 degrees off course, or ran too deep. Follow-up strikes found only one crippled cruiser and a destroyer to finish off, though VF-11 added to its tally later in the day when an Oscar and a Tojo were shot down by Lieutenants (jg) W.H. Boring and L.S. Hardy.

* **Cyr would become CO of CAG-11 in 1960-61.**

Strikes against Japanese fleet units continued for the next two days. Attacking warships near Panay, Sun Downers damaged two light cruisers and a destroyer on the 26th, the same day the skipper notched his first victory. Fairfax and Ensign H.H. Moore each shot down a Jake floatplane for the squadron's 49th and 50th kills of the tour; only five short of the 1943 record. Fourteen search sorties were flown on the 27th as Admiral McCain tried to locate more of the widely-dispersed Japanese fleet, but the VF-11 teams found nothing remarkable. Ensign Charles R. Bratcres spun in during launch and stood up in his cockpit to signal he was all right. But after the F6F sank a rescue destroyer found only his back pack; he was probably snarled on the Hellcat's tail when it went down. The next day Task Group 38.1 headed for Ulithi and a short rest, departing again on November 2.

A new series of strikes was planned to begin November 5, but operational losses still mounted. While landing the morning CAP on the 3rd, Ensign John McVeigh spun in and was killed. He was the thirteenth VF-11 pilot lost in less than one month, the fourth in an accident unrelated to combat.

November 5, 1944, would be the biggest day in the long history of the Sun Downers. In two large dogfights around Clark Field, VF-11 shot down twenty-six planes for the loss of one plane and pilot in combat. At 0615 Gene Fairfax led eleven F6Fs off **Hornet** as part of a large fighter sweep, and eight more as strike 1A against Clark. In all, Fairfax had eighty-seven aircraft from three carriers, including fifty-two Hellcats from **Hornet, Wasp** and **Monterey.** The elements of seven squadrons quickly formed up and headed west towards Manila, 160 miles away.

The fighters dispersed and VF-11 shot up eight twin-engine transports on Tarlac Field, but pilots reported six of these were badly damaged from earlier attacks and may have been left out as dummies. Fairfax then led his divisions south to Mabalacat where Jim Swope noticed aircraft taking off. Blake Moranville, the aggressive young Nebraskan, tallyhoed a Betty far below, rolled over and made a fast overhead run on it. He knew he hit it solidly, but overshot and didn't see the result of his attack. His wingman, Ensign Eddie Kearns, saw the Betty crash.

A large dogfight broke out as Oscars and Tojos appeared. Moranville pulled up to 4,000 feet and got a Tojo but then his guns jammed. He left the hassle to see if he could clear his guns when he spotted a lone Tojo fleeing low on the deck. "I decided I'd better get him before he saw me," Moranville said, and dived down behind him. "Rabbit" fired with only one gun operable, but it was enough. The Tojo caught a wingtip on the ground, cartwheeled and disintegrated.

Meanwhile, the rest of the squadron was having a turkey shoot. Fairfax, Swope, Ensign Jack Suddreth and Lieutenant (jg) Mike South all got two Tojos while five others bagged three more Tojos and two Oscars. The one loss was due as much to equipment as to enemy fighters. Lieutenant Bill Sisley was flying an F6F-3 without water injection while his wingman, Ensign W.M. Mann, flew an

VF-11 Hellcat, GINGER 13, is loaded with a pair of 500-pounders and an auxiliary fuel tank. (H.B. Moranville)

F6F-5P photo plane. An Oscar attacked Mann, setting his belly on fire. Sisley turned into the Oscar but could not get close enough for accurate firing because his dash three lacked sufficient speed. He fired at long range and though the Oscar broke off, Mann was killed. Fairfax regrouped the Sun Downers and established a CAP over the strike area, then escorted the thirty-five bombers back to the task force. VF-11 had bagged sixteen confirmed and two probables.

Hornet's Strike Baker had launched at 0900 and because of the opposition encountered by Fairfax's Strike Able, joined several **Wasp** Hellcats of VF-14 and proceeded on a sweep to Clark Field. The formation arrived over Mt. Arayat about 1015 and seeing several Oscars below, dived to the attack. Jim Savage relates the encounter:

"Several Jap fighters were tally-hoed below and Lieutenant Charlie Stimpson's and my divisions acted as high cover while Lieutenant Commander Bob Clements and a division from VF-14 of the **USS Wasp** went down a few thousand feet and engaged them, shooting down four enemy planes very quickly. Things were quiet after that and Bob came back up to 15,000 feet and joined Charlie and me.

"We milled around a while before I decided to make a strafing run over the field and see what would happen. Bob and his planes had gone up north to look over a few small fields, leaving Charlie and me at Clark. My division, composed of myself and Lieutenant (jg) Walter Boring,

Charlie Stimpson (standing) and Jim Swope examine recon photos for future targets. (Mrs. M.B. Stimpson)

Lieutenant D.T. Work, and Ensign J.E. Olson, made the first pass and I was surprised to see the AA fire close as I entered the dive. We pulled out at 1,000 feet doing some 380 knots. Ensign Olson, who had just joined my division and was on his first combat mission, reported a Jap plane on his tail. I turned sharply away from Olson to let him pass by my position, before turning back toward him and settling down behind the Jap Oscar. I scared him off Olson with tracers, firing out of range. The Jap turned and twisted, diving for the deck and I followed, waiting for a good shot. He straightened out momentarily and I settled down dead astern and just as I started firing a Hellcat came between me and the Jap in an overhead run. It was Olson. I settled down again and put the pipper right on the elevator and fired a good long burst. Pieces started coming off the Oscar and he flamed immediately, hitting the ground and disintegrating.

"As he flamed, I saw another Oscar approaching from the port beam. I turned steeply, but Lieutenant (jg) Boring flamed him before I could get in position. As my wingman, he followed me closely. I turned back into a Jap on the starboard beam and he dove for the deck. I fired a few bursts but missed. He cut throttle and as I overshot with my throttle all the way off, I fired all the way up to his tail, and as I pulled up to miss him he exploded.

"I started for the rally point but was jumped by two more from above. I got a ninety degree shot at one but missed. The other turned away as if to run and I jumped on his tail and finally shot him

Sun Downer aces in the ward room pantry of <u>Hornet</u> talk shop: (l. to r.) Jim Swope (10 victories), Charlie Stimpson (16), and Blake Moranville (6). (H.B. Moranville)

VF-11 Hellcats are barely visible on the deck sinking a Japanese ammo transport off Subic Bay, Philippines, by strafing on 19 November 1944. Avenger torpedo bombers from *Hornet* pass over the action. (E.G. Fairfax)

down after a chase at tree-top level down a road near Clark Field. I again started for the rally point and made a run on another Oscar and fired all my ammo without seeing him go down. I quickly formed my and Charlie's division and headed for home.

"We got ten Jap planes and nobody was scratched. I got three, Lieutenant D.T. Work two, Lieutenant (jg) Boring one, Lieutenant Charles Stimpson three and Ensign Paul Hintz one. Lieutenant Commander Bob Clements division also got four. The day's score for VF-11 was twenty-nine to one, much better than at Formosa. We were getting experience and confidence."

The only other loss of the day came at noon when Ensign Matt Crehan, waiting to land aboard, had to ditch astern of the ship. He was rescued by destroyer **Blue**, mindful that four other **Hornet** fighter pilots had been lost in similar circumstances.

Sweeps and strikes continued for the next two weeks but relatively little air combat resulted. Sun Downers splashed three snoopers on the 13th, though two Oscars bounced Swope's division while escorting Commander Riera and badly shot up Ensign Charley Boineau's F6F. He landed aboard without the use of his flaps. Charlie Stimpson made his last two kills on the 14th with a Zeke and a Tony, the only pilot to score that day. "Rabbit" Moranville became the sixth VF-11 ace when he shot down a Dinah on the 19th while Ensign J.V. Pavela got a Betty.

Bob Saggau, the former All-American, diverted to Tacloban airdrome after an anti-shipping strike on November 10 due to a worrisome oil pressure reading. "As MacArthur had just landed on Leyte I thought I might have the chance to tell him what the *real* war was about," Saggau recalled. But the only person he talked to was the G.I. jeep driver who led him to the parking area. It turned out that both were from the same county in Iowa.

On November 20 **Hornet's** task group prepared to return to Ulithi, but twenty-six junior pilots were transferred with aircraft to other carriers. Though some of them eventually rejoined VF-11, it was a shock to the squadron and Gene Fairfax looked upon it as the loss of a large part of his family. While in Ulithi for three weeks, however, VF-11's pilot strength was doubled as a matter of policy in the Fast Carrier Task Force. After the appearance of Kamikazes in the Philippines, increased demands on fighter squadrons resulted in authorized strength being established at 105 pilots and about 75 aircraft. Consequently, in early December the Sun Downers received two more Lieutenant commanders; Fritz E. Wolf and Edward H. Bayers. Wolf was a combat-experienced veteran of the American Volunteer Group in the CBI Theater of 1941-42, where he was credited with two and one-half confirmed victories. Bayers was an old friend of Bob Clements, who described him as 'the best fighter pilot I ever knew."

Clements might have obtained his own command at this time, as some air groups were dividing their enlarged fighter squadrons into two units, one designated a fighter-bomber outfit. Emmett Riera and Gene Fairfax discussed the situation and decided there was no need to change; Clements agreed. With more missions to be flown, the workload remained the same for each division, and administration proved no major problem.

Sun Downers tell their war stories to correspondents aboard Hornet. (L. to R.) H.E. Maring, Blake Moranville, A.J. Engle, Keith Wheeler (Chicago Sun Times) Bill Marion (Australian News Service). (H.B. Moranville)

"Rabbit" Moranville (left), Jim Swope and Squadron mascot, Gunner, take a nap in the ready room. (H. B. Moranville)

The fast carriers returned briefly to the Philippines where a series of strikes was flown from December 13 to 16. Four more aerial victories were added to VF-11's total during this period, making eighty-seven to date for the West Pac deployment. Jimmie Savage recalls the mission of the 15th:

"Took off from the **Hornet** on a photo and escort mission. Target was Del Carmen Field located south of Clark. We approached at 13,000 feet with no opposition except AA. I made my photo runs as our VB and VT did the bombing. After I had taken the required pictures, I made a rocket run on some parked planes and pulled out toward the rally point. I heard a 'tally-ho' and upon looking down I spotted a Judy low and forty-five degrees to my port side. I swung around and gave full throttle to catch him but Lieutenant A.J. Meyer, Norfolk, Virginia, was already shooting at him. I throttled back, and as Meyer overran him, I closed to 900 feet and opened fire. He took evasive action by turning and slipping and the pilot threw out a parachute which passed just under my wing. I flamed him then at about fifty feet off the deck, and as he exploded on the ground a wheel came up higher than my plane at the time.

"We formed our flight and returned to the **Hornet** after searching the east coast for a downed pilot."

Flight operations completely ceased on the 17th and much of the 18th due to a terrific typhoon. During the height of the storm two destroyers astern of **Hornet** rolled over and sank. Search missions were flown for crippled ships enroute back to Ulithi where the task force spent the holidays.

Hornet exercised her aircraft in predawn operations on January 1, 1945, and then headed west again to the now familiar hunting grounds of Formosa. In a predawn mission on the third, Gene Fairfax led two divisions against Tainan during which he spotted a Mavis flying boat low on the water, providing anti-submarine protection for a convoy. Fairfax and his wingman, Jack Suddreth, both attacked unsuccessfully before Jim Swope exploded it. Later in the day VF-11 damaged a transport and an oiler.

By January 6 the task force was back in the Philippines, with sweeps over Mabalacat and Bambam airfields. Two Zekes were shot down and two more claimed as probables, bringing the Sun Downers' total to ninety destroyed in the air. Next day saw more combat over the same area, during which Lieutenant (jg) John Sims lost formation in some heavy clouds never to be seen again. The second of the morning's strikes encountered Zekes and Tojos, with Henry White claiming two of the latter to become the last Sun Downer ace. Jake Robcke also bagged a Zeke, but Ensign James H. Bethel, Jr. was killed when he tried to follow a Zeke in a split-S from eight hundred feet. Other pilots reported that Bethel

On December 17, 1944 a typhoon caught Task Force 38 between the Philippines and Ulithi, curtailing flight operations. Some aircraft were wrenched loose from <u>Hornet</u>'s deck. (Mrs. M.B. Stimpson)

hadn't even reached the vertical when his Hellcat hit the water. That afternoon another F6F was lost when Lieutenant (jg) M.J. Hayter ran out of fuel, but Hayter was rescued.

Two days later the Sun Downers were back at Formosa for a highly-successful anti-shipping strike. Commander Riera led a division which sank a destroyer escort while Lieutenant Commander Ed Bayers' division was largely responsible for another destroyer. A 10,000-ton oiler and 3,000 ton transport were also sunk by bombs and rockets while three more ships of 16,000 gross tons were badly damaged.

During the night of January 11-12, Task Force 38 entered the South China Sea for the first carrier strike on French Indo-China. Fairfax's pilots flew four strikes and two sweeps during the 12th in addition to CAP and photo flights. Two destroyer escorts were sunk in Camranh Bay, one by the proficient team of Ed Bayers and Ensign F.C.

This sequence shows a Japanese warship being attacked off the coast of French Indo-China on January 12, 1945 by VF-11. An explosion on the stern causes the ship to go dead in the water and eventually to sink, stern first. From the profile it is possible that she was the British mine sweeper Taitam, seized by the Japanese on the marine ways at Hong Kong in December 1941. Japanese records indicate that she was sunk in this location by aircraft of Task Force 38. (Mrs. M.B. Stimpson)

Onion. Five other destroyers were damaged, as were two transports.

No enemy aircraft were encountered by the Sun Downers, but for the first and last time a VF-11 ace was lost in combat. On the second sweep "Rabbit" Moranville's F6F was hit by 20 mm while rocketing Tan Son Nhut airport. Though Blake had once brought a badly shot-up F6F back to **Hornet**, and broke his arresting hook on landing, he knew the Pratt & Whitney would burn itself out in a few minutes. He had no choice but to look for a suitable landing spot.

The four Hellcats of Swopes' flight were now low over the Southern portion of the Mekong Delta, crossing numerous streams and tributaries, still heading southwest. Oil pressure in Moranville's F6F was almost zero; temperature well in the red. Abruptly the engine seized tight; the three-bladed propeller wrenched to a halt. Blake picked up a large rice paddy on the north bank of the Song Hau River and turned to set up his approach.

Canopy back and locked, magneto switch off, fuel off, shoulder harness extra tight, Blake reached over to his left and dropped his arresting hook. When he got down to the last few feet the hook would drag along the surface, telling him he was close enough to stall the Hellcat in. He had a good long approach, allowing ample time to set up his glide angle and decided to keep the flaps up until he cleared the near row of trees. He noticed a large number of people standing on the dikes which surrounded the paddy and fleetingly assumed they were peasants, but then was concentrating on his landing.

Lieutenant Commander Gene Fairfax was skipper of VF-11 for the second tour of combat. (E.G. Fairfax)

When he cleared the trees Blake dropped his flaps and kept milking the stick back as the blunt nose came up. He felt the tail hook grabbing at the water. That was it; he brought the stick clear back and the Hellcat splashed down smoothly with hardly a jolt. Blake didn't know it, but he was some seventy-five statute miles southwest of Saigon, between the village of Tra On and Cau Ke.

Blake flipped the IFF destruct switch on the electrical panel to prevent the Japanese from learning the transponder's frequency should they find **Ginger 30**. Then he unbuckled his seat belt and shoulder harness and stood up in the cockpit. He had an impression of Swope and the others still overhead but paid them little attention. With his parachute still strapped on, Blake climbed out and stepped from the wing into the knee-deep water. He sloshed past the nose of the Hellcat, and though he didn't stop to look closely, saw that small arms fire had struck the propeller governor. Otherwise he saw little damage except one wingtip slightly dented from the landing. Blake didn't learn until years later about the 20 mm hole in his cowling, as it was hidden below the water.

Still circling overhead, Jim Swope was keeping an eye on the downed plane and pilot. "Blake was a lonely looking figure, standing in the rice paddy by his airplane," Swope said, "and all three of us would have landed alongside him if we had thought it would help." But that was impossible so they did the next best thing to help their friend. Swope opened his canopy and tossed out his emergency packet of money — Bank of Shanghai Gold Notes — in hopes Blake could use it. Kearns and Boineau did the same, but Blake never saw the packets falling into the paddy. After a few more moments, the three F6Fs set course back to **Hornet**.

Blake turned and started walking toward the edge of the paddy, wondering what he was going to do next. It was rough going with the chute still strapped on and . . . that was it! The one thing he'd forgotten before splashing down. He hadn't taken off his parachute harness as a part of the ditching procedure.

Blake turned in his tracks and slogged back to the plane. He took off the chute and laid it carefully on the wing. All aviators were taught from primary training until the day they received their wings that parachutes are lifesaving devices and should always be treated as such. Blake had just set his chute down, keeping the straps from dangling in the water, when he stood upright and almost shouted aloud, "What am I doing?" Obviously, the chute was no longer important to his survival. He should have just dropped it in the water; he was wasting precious time. He considered burning the Hellcat to deprive the Japanese of it, but decided he'd better get out of the area immediately.

Mad at himself ("I had other things on my mind," he would recall) Blake got across the paddy and climbed

Sun Downers at rest, playing bridge in the ready room. (l. to r.) Eddie Kearns, Charlie Stimpson, Jim Swope, Charlie Boineau. (H.B. Moranville)

up an embankment and started walking, not really knowing where he wanted to go. He had a vague notion that if he could somehow get to the Philippines he'd be all right. Then suddenly he was surrounded by people on top of the dike. He considered reaching for the .38 caliber revolver under his left arm, but recognized the people as Annamites. The were obviously the same ones he'd seen during the final moments in the air. Blake stared at them for a minute and they stared back. Not knowing what else to do, he began speaking slowly, asking for assistance but getting no response. He tried a few more times before he thought he heard a small boy say something in English.

Blake concentrated on the boy, who proved reluctant to talk, but eventually the lad admitted he spoke broken English. Following more lengthy discourse the boy and an old man agreed to lead Blake to safety. They took him to a peasant house and gave him a bottle of soda water before continuing on. After another hour's walk they neared a small village and Blake pulled up short. He suspected a trap, figuring he was being delivered to the Japanese. But he had nowhere else to go, and as a precaution unsnapped the strap over the handle of his .38. The boy saw this movement and shook his head: "No, no. No worry." Blake nodded and they continued on, but the pilot remained wary. "If these characters are leading me into a trap," he thought, "the Japs may get me but I'll get these two."

The boy and the old man took Blake to the village church and then left. Many of the villagers came by to look at the stranger but didn't bother him. As it was nearly dark, Blake settled down to try and get some sleep but couldn't doze off. He'd been there about ninety minutes when he heard a car drive up and, tense and alert, saw a white man in civilian clothes enter the church.

"I am French," the man said, explaining in fairly fluent English that he was magistrate of the area, and gave Blake some cognac. He had come to take the American aviator to a place of safety if Lieutenant Moranville would care to step into the vehicle parked outside. Once again, things seemed to be decided for him so Blake went to the Frenchman's car, a coal-burning automobile. It was the first he'd ever seen, and the official explained that gasoline was in short supply in Indo-China these days. "The war, you know."

Thus began Blake Moranville's two-and-one-half month saga of escape and evasion in French Indo China (later Vietnam). Sheltered by both the native population and the French colonial administration from occupying Japanese forces, Moranville was spirited from one location to another, finally participating with the French in a fighting retreat to Dien Bien Phu. With six other American airmen he was eventually airlifted out of Vietnam by U.S. Army Intelligence and units of General Chennault's Fourteenth Air Force as Japanese forces closed in on Dien Bien Phu.

On the day that Blake Moranville went down concern was somewhat alleviated by the fact that "Rabbit" was seen safely walking around his plane, but Gunner the mascot was despondent over the loss of his master.

Jim Swope, shown in his F6F-3, scored 4 2/3 victories at Guadalcanal and five more by the end of the <u>Hornet</u> tour. (National Archives via Charles Graham)

Happily, they were reunited several months later in Nebraska.

On the morning of January 15th, VF-11 launched sweeps against Formosa while Gene Fairfax took two of his own divisions and four from other squadrons for a look at Hong Kong. About fifty miles east of the target area, Fairfax noticed a Tabby transport, a Japanese-built DC-3, escorted by four Zekes. This indicated an important passenger aboard the Tabby, and the C.O. instructed his pilots to "Leave the transport alone until we have the escorts." Fairfax, Jake Robcke, Ensign H.H. Moore and Ensign J.P. Wolf each got a Zeke, then Fairfax and "Soapy" Suddreth went after Tabby. "We probably overkilled it," Fairfax said, and the only way to decide credit was to flip a coin. It was a squadron policy not to split a kill, and Suddreth won the toss. The Tabby went in the records as his third victory; Fairfax now had four. The only other aerial victory on the 15th was a Jill downed by Jim Swope, his fifth kill of the tour and tenth of the war.

1. Correspondence with E.G. Fairfax, 1976. Dr. Alvin Coox of San Diego State University established the VIP's identity as Vice Admiral K. Hatakeyama, on an inspection of Japanese defenses in Southern China.

VF-11 pilots pose on Hornet. (l. to r.) Matt Crehan (one of the last to be downed) Jim Crowley, Bob Clements, exec., Clyde Parsley and J.J. McCarron. (J.J. Crowley)

The Sun Downers are awarded a cake by the Hornet for operations with no "wave offs". Squadron CO Gene Fairfax holds the cake. Clockwise, from Fairfax, the pilots are: Lawrence Hardy, Richard Cyr, Sol White, James S. Brown, Bob Clements (exec), George Morris, Emmett Riera (CAG), Walton Boring, Charles Stimpson, Charles Boineau, John Ramsey, Oscar West, Jack Suddreth. (E.G. Fairfax)

37

Commander R.E. Riera, skipper of CAG-11, flew Hellcat No. 52. (B. Tillman)

Next day the squadron was back over Hong Kong in force, suffering two losses from fifty-four sweep and strike sorties. A 10,000-ton oiler was severely damaged by an estimated twelve rocket hits while Charlie Stimpson's division set afire the oil storage area and Cac Flath's pilots worked over Kowloon Docks. Ensign Matt Crehan's Hellcat was damaged by flak over the harbor on Strike Charlie and he bailed out near Tamkan Island while his division leader, Bob Clements, circled overhead.

With no other Hellcats in the area, Clements got hold of a bomber pilot who dropped a life raft, as Crehan's raft had drifted away. But it failed to inflate so Clements somehow managed to drop his own, and Crehan climbed in. Calling for a rescue submarine, Clements meanwhile scared away fishing boats and sampans until his ammunition ran out, only to discover the sub couldn't go in close enough to shore. The conscientious exec remained overhead until his radio quit and he had thirty gallons of fuel remaining. He sweated all the way back to **Hornet**, landing with the gauge reading empty. Crehan was not found by subsequent searches and therefore appeared in the VF-11 cruise book among those killed in action. Not till after the war did Clements learn from Crehan himself that the young Bay Stater had been fished out of the water by friendly Chinese who helped him get to Kunming, where he met Blake Moranville. It was a small war.

But it was still a shooting war, and Ensign Richard Wilson fell to AA fire during strike 1-D. He was the seventeenth and last Sun Downer killed during the deployment.

After Hong Kong it was back to Formosa on January 21, 1945. Five support vessels totaling 25,000 tons were damaged, as were two destroyers. In the squadron's final dogfight, Lieutenant W.R. Sisley led Ensigns Knott, Williams and McReynolds into a formation of Zekes and Judys. Knott splashed a Judy and the others each got a Zeke. One more Hellcat was lost when Lieutenant Commander Fritz Wolf splashed down after launch with zero oil pressure but was rescued by a destroyer. The next day VF-11 flew its last combat missions of the war against targets on Okinawa.

From October 10, 1944 to January 22, 1945, the Sun Downers were credited with 103 Japanese aircraft shot down and sixteen probables in addition to 288 destroyed on the ground. A destroyer and three destroyer escorts were sunk with twenty-one similar vessels damaged to varying extents. Over 27,000 tons of merchant shipping was sunk by Fairfax's Hellcats and nearly 180,000 tons damaged. Excluding aircraft damaged beyond local repair, VF-11 lost twenty-seven F6Fs including twelve to operational causes. Eight were shot down by AA fire and seven in aerial combat; a total of fifteen lost to enemy action. Pilot losses amounted to twenty, including Commander Schrader who was killed and Moranville and Crehan who both safely returned to the U.S. Of these, the seven lost in air combat represented the single largest cause while five were killed by anti-aircraft fire. Two pilots were lost to unknown causes but both were believed inflicted by enemy action; DeRolf near Manila and Sims over Luzon. Additionally, the **Hornet** night fighter detachment lost one pilot and two aircraft in accidents but

Charlie Stimpson in the cockpit of his Hellcat near the end of VF-11's second tour of combat. (National Archives via Charles Graham)

these casualties were not attributed to VF-11. **Hornet** and her squadrons were awarded the Presidential Unit Citation for actions during VF-11's deployment.

The 103 victories scored under Gene Fairfax established VF-11 as the 17th ranked Hellcat squadron among over eighty which flew F6Fs in combat. Thus the seven Sun Downer Hellcats known lost in aerial combat resulted in a kill-loss ratio of nearly fifteen to one. But one fact the Sun Downers could be particularly proud of was that no Air Group 11 dive bomber or torpedo plane was lost to enemy aircraft. From 1943 to 1945 VF-11s box score was 158 aerial victories against seventeen Grummans and eleven pilots lost in air combat. Charlie Stimpson set the pace on both tours with a total of sixteen, followed by Jim Swope with ten. Then came Doc Savage with seven, Blake Moranville with six and Bob Clements, Vern Graham and Henry White with five each. These seven aces accounted for fifty-four victories or over one-third of the total. Sun Downers had shot down a variety of fifteen Japanese aircraft types, headed by sixty-five Zekes or Hamps, twenty-six Tojos, twenty Vals, nineteen Oscars and ten Judys.

Fairfax took Jim Swope to NAS Los Alamitos when he assumed command of VF-98, the West Coast fighter training squadron, and Doc Savage went to VBF-98. Swope and Cyr later went to VF-66 and flew the Ryan FR-1 Fireball. Blake Moranville rejoined VF-11 briefly at NAS Fallon, Nevada for a boisterous three-day reunion in Reno and finished the war as an instrument instructor. Bob Clements returned to the Naval Academy.

In 1948 the Squadron was redesignated VF-11A, and in 1956 VF-111 in accordance with a Navy-wide designation system change. But subsequent Navy fliers carried the Sun Downer name into two more wars.

Flying Grumman F9F Panthers, the squadron flew three tours of combat in the Korean War, winning another Distinguished Unit Citation and claiming the Navy's first jet kill, a North Korean MiG-15.

Some eighteen years later the next air to air tally, a MiG-21, was scored with a missile by a VF-111 team flying a Vought F8U Crusader over North Vietnam. The squadron participated in a total of seven deployments during the Vietnam conflict, converting along the way to the McDonnell F-4 Phantom and scoring another MiG-17 victory in 1972.

From the Vietnam war until today the Sun Downers have continued to serve the nation in a restless peace. As this history is published the squadron is again mounted in Grumman aircraft, flying F-14 Tomcats off **Kitty Hawk** in the Persian Gulf.

In 1946 their first combat commander, Clarence White (now deceased) reflected, "Fighting the peace is not half as much fun as fighting the war. The chaos is so much more disorganized." A legion of Sun Downers from 1943 to this day would doubtless say, "Amen to that, Skipper."

The PA system on <u>Hornet</u> announces, "Pilots, man your planes," as, once more, the Sun Downers head for their Hellcats. (Mrs. M.B. Stimpson)

Awards ceremony for VF-11 pilots. Charlie Stimpson is shown receiving his second Navy Cross and clusters to the DFC. (Mrs. M.B. Stimpson)

AVIATION MECH

You may laud your medals bright when you're in the bar at night
And the curvy waitress brings them cold with foam.
But when you're combat fly'n and ship is really try'n,
It's the ground crewmen that really bring you home.

Of all the fighting crew, the finest men I knew
Were the good ole grinning, growling, aviation mechs.
Working long into the night to make her fly just right,
His one reward - a thumbs up sign from me.

I shan't forget the day we zoomed into the fray,
When a Zero latched himself upon my tail.
Though dive and twist and turn, I was soon to learn
My acrobatics were to no avail.

With one chance to stay alive, I rolled into a dive
And pushed the throttle forward through the "gate".
She had the speed to go, if the engine didn't blow,
Mechanic's skill did then control my fate.

So I wear my ribbons proud and tell my stories loud,
Describing smoking guns and bursting flak,
But the man not in the story - the one deserving glory -
Is the good ole grinning, growling aviation mech.

Originally written by AAF pilot, Ken Lashbrook. Revised by Vernon S. Graham, VF-11

APPENDIX A

FIRST COMBAT TOUR

PILOT ROSTER

AERIAL CLAIMS

RANK	NAME	CONF.	PROB.	DAM.	REMARKS
Lt. (jg)	C.G. Boswell				KIA
Lt. Cdr.	G.D. Cady	1	1		
Lt. (jg)	C.G. Cary	1			KIA
Ens.	L.W. Childs				KIA
Lt. (jg)	J.A. Cooke	1	1		
Lt. (jg)	E.M. Coppola	1			Also VF-14
Lt. (jg)	R.N. Flath				
Lt. (jg)	V.W. Gaston	1.66			
Lt. (jg)	R.L. Gilbert	3		2	
Lt. (jg)	V.E. Graham	5			
Lt.	W.J. Hiebert	1			
Lt. (jg)	T.H. Holberton	2			
Ens.	W.D. Hubbard				
Ens.	D.R. Hubler				
Lt. (jg)	T.L. Hull	2			KIA
Ens.	C.M. Ivie	1			
Lt. (jg)	E.H. Johnson				KPC in U.S.
Lt. (jg)	A.A. Jones				
Lt.	W.N. Leonard	2			
Ens.	B.J. Martin				
Lt. (jg)	W.J. Masoner	2			Also VF-19
Lt. (jg)	W.R. Maxwell				Also VF-51
Lt. (jg)	R.B. Ogilvie				
Lt. (jg)	C.A. Parker	1			
Lt. (jg)	A.T. Pimentel	1			
Lt. (jg)	J.G. Pressler	2			
Lt.	F.B. Quady	2	1		Also VF-6
Lt. (jg)	J.W. Ramsey	2			
Lt. (jg)	G.W. Ricker				KIA
Lt. (jg)	C.H. Schild	3			
Lt. (jg)	L.E. Slagle				
Lt. (jg)	C.R. Stimpson	6			
Lt. (jg)	J.S. Swope	4.66			
Lt. (jg)	K.T. Viall	4		1	
Lt. Cdr.	R.W. Vogel	1			
Lt.	L.S. Wall, Jr.				
Lt.	C.V.M. Wesley	2			
Lt. Cdr.	C.M. White	.66	2		
Lt. (jg)	H.S. White	2			
Lt. (jg)	D.T. Work				
		55	5	3	

Glossary of Terms
KIA Killed in Action
KOA Killed in Operating Accident
KPC Killed in Plane Crash

APPENDIX B
SECOND COMBAT TOUR
PILOT ROSTER

AERIAL CLAIMS

RANK	NAME	CONF.	PROB.	DAM.	REMARKS
Ens.	G.G. Anderson	1			KIA
Ens.	A.M. Ball				
Lt. Cdr.	E.H. Bayers				Also VF-6 &VF-3
Ens.	B.K. Beckwith				
Ens.	J.S. Bethel				KIA
Ens.	P. Bilbao				
Ens.	F.J.C. Blair	3			KIA
Ens.	C.E. Boineau	1			
Ens.	D.R. Borgeson				Also VBF-3
Lt. (jg)	W.H. Boring	3			
Ens.	H.E. Brookens				
Lt.	J.S. Brown	1			
Ens.	C.R. Bratcres				KOA
Ens.	J.R. Byerly				
Lt. Cdr.	G.D. Cady				KOA TF38
Ens.	F.R. Chapman, Jr.				Also VBF-17
Ens.	K.C. Chase				KIA
Lt. Cdr.	R.E. Clements	5			
Ens.	E.G. Clouser				
Lt. (jg)	G.A. Coeur	1			
Ens.	M.J. Crehan				Downed, evaded
Ens.	F.W. Crowell				Also VF-3
Ens.	J.J. Crowley				
Lt.	K.G. Crusoe	1			Also VF-18
Lt.	R.F. Cyr	4	2		Also VB-11
Ens.	R.C. Dance	1			
Lt.	N.W. Dayhoff	2			KIA
Ens.	W. DeRolf				KIA
Ens.	D.R. DeWitt				Also VF-19
Ens.	C. Dikoff				Also VBF-17
Lt. (jg)	W.G. Eccles	1			Also VF-18
Ens.	G.E. Edling				Also VBF-17
Ens.	N.W. Eft				
Lt. (jg)	A.J. Engle				
Lt. Cdr.	E.G. Fairfax	4			
Ens.	R.P. Farley	2			
Lt.	R.N. Flath	1			
Ens.	W.L. Garlic		1		Also VF-19
Lt. (jg)	S.E. Goldberg				KIA
Ens.	R. Grosso				Also VBF-17
Ens.	A.R. Groves				
Lt. (jg)	L.S. Hardy, Jr.	1			
Lt. (jg)	M.J. Hayter				Also VF-18
Ens.	E.E. Helgerson				KOA
Lt. (jg)	P.F. Hintze				
Ens.	O.L. Jacobsen				

APPENDIX B (Cont.)

AERIAL CLAIMS

RANK	NAME	CONF.	PROB.	DAM.	REMARKS
Lt.	T.H. Holberton				
Lt. (jg)	C.W. James	1	1		
Lt. (jg)	N.L. Jeffers				Also VF-7
Ens.	B.V. Jesmer				Also VF-3
Ens.	P.E. King				
Ens.	W.E. Kearns	1			
Ens.	Z.V. Knott	2			
Ens.	W.J. Koressel				
Ens.	L.E. Lee				KOA
Ens.	T. Lepianka				
Ens.	R.K. Lewis				
Ens.	G.E. Lindesmith	1			KIA
Ens.	W.E. Lizotte	2			
Ens.	W.M. Mann				KIA
Ens.	S.J. Manning	1			Also VF-7 & VF-20
Ens.	J. Mansfield				
Lt.	H.E. Maring				
Ens.	W.H. Martin, Jr.				Also VF-19
Lt.	R. McBride	2			
Ens.	J.J. McCarron		1		
Ens.	R. McReynolds				
Ens.	J.J. McVeigh				KOA
Lt.	A.R. Meyer	2			
Ens.	A.T. Miles				Also VF-3
Lt. (jg)	H.B. Moranville	6			Downed, evaded.
Ens.	A.W. Morriss, III	1			
Lt.	G.L. Morris, Jr.		1		
Ens.	H.H. Moore	2		1	
Lt.	R.W. Moore				Also VBF-17
Ens.	J.A. Mudd				
Ens.	R.A. Nelson				
Ens.	W.H. Nowlin				
Lt.	E.S. Ogle				
Ens.	J.E. Olson	1			
Ens.	F.C. Onion				Also VF-3
Lt. (jg)	C.L. Parsley	1	1		
Ens.	J.V. Pavela	1			
Ens.	H. Ptacek				KIA
Lt.	J.W. Ramsey	2			
Ens.	S.J. Richardson				
Cdr.	E. Riera				
Ens.	J.H. Robcke	3			
Ens.	K.M. Roberts				Also VF-15
Ens.	W.C. Robinson				Also VBF-3
Lt. (jg)	H.M. Rowland, Jr.				Also VF-3
Lt.	R.J. Saggau				Also VB-11
Ens.	L.B. Sahm				
Lt.	J.E. Savage	7	1		
Ens.	F.T. Scharrer				Also VBF-3

APPENDIX B (Cont.)

AERIAL CLAIMS

RANK	NAME	CONF.	PROB.	DAM.	REMARKS
Cdr.	F.R. Schrader				KIA
Lt. (jg)	J.P. Sims				KIA
Lt.	W.R. Sisley	2	1		
Ens.	C.D. Smith				
Ens.	H.E. Smith				
Lt. (jg)	M.P South	2			
Lt.	C.R. Stimpson	10	2		
Ens.	H.J. Stockert				Also VF-2
Ens.	J.M. Suddreth	3	1		
Lt.	J.S. Swope	5	2		
Ens.	T.W. Tidwell				
Ens.	T.C. Tillar				Also VF-2 and VF-7
Ens.	A.P. Tonsfeldt				
Ens.	R.C. Vance				
Lt.	B.L. Voegle		1		
Ens.	K.K. Walker				
Ens.	P.C. Warren				
Lt. (jg)	J. Welder	1			
Lt.	J.S. Welfelt				
Lt.	O.H. West, Jr.	1			
Lt.	H.S. White	3			
Ens.	J.R. Whiteside				
Lt. (jg)	T. St.C. Williams	1			
Lt. (jg)	J.T. Williss				Also VF-18
Ens.	R.E. Wilson				KIA
Lt. Cdr.	F.E. Wolf				Also VBF-3
Ens.	J.P. Wolf	1			
Lt.	D.T. Work	3	1	1	
Lt.(jg)	J.A. Zink	3			Also VF-18 and VF-7
Lt.	W.O. Zoecklein				
		103	16	2	

APPENDIX C
ACES ASSOCIATED WITH VF-11

NAME	1ST TOUR	2ND TOUR	WITH OTHER UNITS	TOTAL
Robert E. Clements	0	5		5
Vernon E. Graham	5	-		5
William N. Leonard	2	-	4 with VF-42 and VF-3	6
William E. Masoner	2	-	10 with VF-19	12
William R. Maxwell	0	-	7 with VF-51	7
H. Blake Moranville	-	6		6
Jimmie E. Savage	-	7		7
Charles R. Stimpson	6	10		16
James S. Swope	4.66	5		9.66
Henry S. White	2	3		5
John A. Zink	-	3	2 with VF-18 and VF-7	5

APPENDIX D
PLANE TYPES ASSIGNED TO VF-11/VF-111

1942-1943	F4F-4
1944-1945	F6F-3/5
Dec. 1946	F8F-1
Mar. 1949	F8F-2
Dec. 1949	F9F-2
Sep. 1952	F9F-5
Dec. 1953	F9F-6
Jun. 1955	F9F-8
Jun. 1957	FJ-3
Jan. 1959	F11F-1
May 1961	F-8E
Mar 1968	F-8J
Nov 1969	F-8H
Jan 1971	F-4B
Mar 1974	F-4N
Oct 1978	F-14A

APPENDIX E
DUTY STATIONS AND DEPLOYMENTS VF-11/VF111

STATION	CO	STATION	CO
1943 - Guadalcanal	White	1969 - USS Ticonderoga	Finney
1944-45 - USS Hornet	Fairfax	1970 - USS Shangri-La	Dimon/Rennis
1945 - NAS Fallon/Santa Rosa	Jackson	1971 - USS Coral Sea	Pearl
1946 - Maui	Jackson/Fairfax/Crews	1973 - USS Coral Sea	Rice/Markley
1948 - USS Valley Forge	Rogers	1973 - USS Coral Sea	Markley
1948-49 - San Diego	Flynn	1974 - USS Coral Sea	Brickner
1950 - USS Philippine Sea	Amen	1975 - NAS Miramar	Alexander
1951 - USS Valley Forge	Ramsey	1977 - USS Franklin D. Roosevelt	Clift
1953 - USS Boxer/Lake Champlain	Vickery	1979-80 - USS Kitty Hawk	Hipper/Geeding
1954 - USS Wasp	Knudson	1981 - USS Kitty Hawk	Schmitt
1956 - USS Lexington	Medick	1982 - USS Carl Vinson	Milam
1957 - USS Bennington	Miller	1983 - USS Carl Vinson	Bjerke
1958 - USS Bennington	Huxford	1984 - USS Carl Vinson	McPherson
1959 - USS Shangri-La	Godfrey	1986 - USS Carl Vinson	McPherson
1960 - USS Hancock	Cheal	1987 - USS Carl Vinson	James
1961 - USS Hancock	Winter	1988 - USS Carl Vinson	Rose
1962 - USS Kitty Hawk	Moore	1989 - USS Carl Vinson	MacKenzie
1963 - USS Kitty Hawk	Wellons	1990 - NAS - Miramar	Rollins
1964 - USS Kitty Hawk	Ray	1991 - USS Kitty Hawk	Rollins
1965 - USS Midway	Butler	1992 - USS Kitty Hawk	Clement
1966 - USS Oriskany	Cook	1993 - USS Kitty Hawk/Persian Gulf	Purcell
1967 - USS Oriskany	Rasmussen		

APPENDIX F
VF-11 and VF-111
SUN DOWNER COMMANDING OFFICERS

YEAR	CO	YEAR	CO
10 Oct 1942	LCDR Charles R. Fenton	1963	CDR Charles E. Ray
20 Apr 1943	LCDR Clarence M. White	1965	CDR James La Haye
25 Sep 1943	CDR Gordon D. Cady	1965	CDR Doyle W. Lynn
Mid Aug 1944	LCDR Eugene G. Fairfax	1965	CDR Dempsey Butler, Jr.
9 Apr 1945	Lt George W. Bert (Acting)	1966	CDR Richard M. Cook
21 Apr 1945	LCDR Percival W. Jackson	1967	CDR Robert L. Rasmussen
20 May 1946	LCDR David L. Soper (Acting)	1968	CDR Jack L. Finney
28 May 1946	LCDR Eugene G. Fairfax	1969	CDR Charles G. Dimon
27 Sep 1946	CDR Howard W. Crews	1970	CDR William B. Rennie
6 Jun 1947	LCDR Robert S. Merritt (Acting)	1971	CDR Harlan R. Pearl
20 Jul 1947	CDR Richard S. Rogers	1972	CDR Robert P. Rice
15 Jul 1948	LCDR David R. Flynn	1973	CDR Wade E. Markley
? Jan 1950	LCDR William T. Amen	1974	CDR John S. Brickner
? Jun 1951	CDR Frank Welch, Jr.	1975	CDR H. David Alexander
29 Oct 1951	Lt. H.E. "Red" Hix (Acting)	1977	CDR Thomas A. Clift
8 Nov 1951	LCDR John W. Ramsey	1978	CDR Ira M. Hipper
? Aug 1952	Lt. David W. Henderson (Acting)	1979	CDR Robert W. Geeding
27 Aug 1952	LCDR La Vier C. Alber	1980	CDR Stuart O. Schmitt
1952	CDR Arthur E. Vickery	1982	CDR Lonzo O. Milam
1954	CDR Angus J. Knudson	1984	CDR David G. Bjerke
1955	CDR Glenn A. Medic	1985	CDR Thomas L. McPherson
1955	CDR Frank E. Miller	1986	CDR Lloyd E. James
1958	CDR Richard W. Huxford	1988	CDR Raymond Park Rose
1959	CDR Jack E. Godfrey	1989	CDR Thomas L. MacKenzie
1959	CDR Wayne R. Cheal	1990	CDR Bryan L. Rollins
1961	CDR Homer A. Winter	1992	CDR Robert H. Clement
1962	CDR Robert E. Moore	1993	CDR Marc L. Purcell
1963	LCDR Alfred G. Wellons		

DEFINITIVE MILITARY/AVIATION HISTORIES
By
PHALANX PUBLISHING CO., LTD.

The Pineapple Air Force: Pearl Harbor to Tokyo
by John Lambert $34.95

Republic P-47 Thunderbolt, The Final Chapter: Latin American Air Forces Service
by Dan Hagedorn $10.95

Eagles of Duxford: The 78th Fighter Group in World War II
by Garry Fry $22.95

Kearby's Thunderbolts: The 348th Fighter Group in World War II
by John Stanaway $24.95

Wildcats Over Casablanca
by John Lambert $11.95

B-25 Mitchell, The Magnificent Medium
by Norman L. Avery $29.95

SORTIE:
A bibliography of U.S. Air Force, Navy and Marine combat aviation unit histories from World War II. Compiled by John W. Lambert $10.95

Pacific Air Combat - Voices From The Past
By Henry Sakaida

FORTHCOMING TITLES

MESSERSCHMITT ROULETTE:
The Desert War from a Hurricane Recce Pilot of No 451 Squadron RAAF by Wing Commander Geoffrey Morley-Mower, RAF, (ret.), DFC

THE 1ST FIGHTER GROUP IN WORLD WAR II:
The MTO war of the this legendary P-38 unit by one of its pilots, John D. Mullins

FANTAIL FIGHTERS
U.S. Navy battleship and cruiser floatplanes in World War II, by Jerry Scutts

YANKS FROM YOXFORD
The 357th Fighter Group in Europe by Merle Olmsted

MARINE MITCHELLS
U.S. Marine Corps operations with PBJ aircraft in the Pacific, by Jerry Scutts.